THEOLOGY ON DC

THEOLOGY ON DOVER BEACH

NICHOLAS LASH

Darton, Longman and Todd
London

First published in 1979 by
Darton, Longman and Todd Ltd
89, Lillie Road, London SW6 IUD

ISBN 0 232 51433 X

Printed in Great Britain by The Anchor Press Ltd
and bound by Wm Brendon & Son Ltd
both of Tiptree, Essex

CONTENTS

Dover Beach

The sea is calm tonight.
The tide is full, the moon lies fair
Upon the straits; – on the French coast the light
Gleams and is gone; the cliffs of England stand,
Glimmering and vast, out in the tranquil bay.
Come to the window, sweet is the night-air!
Only, from the long line of spray
Where the sea meets the moon-blanched land,
Listen! you hear the grating roar
Of pebbles which the waves draw back, and fling,
At their return, up the high strand,
Begin, and cease, and then again begin,
With tremulous cadence slow, and bring
The eternal note of sadness in.

Sophocles long ago
Heard it on the Aegean, and it brought
Into his mind the turbid ebb and flow
Of human misery; we
Find also in the sound a thought,
Hearing it by this distant northern sea.

The Sea of Faith
Was once, too, at the full, and round earth's shore
Lay like the folds of a bright girdle furl'd.
But now I only hear
Its melancholy, long, withdrawing roar,
Retreating, to the breath
Of the night-wind, down the vast edges drear
And naked shingles of the world.

Ah, love, let us be true
To one another! for the world, which seems
To lie before us like a land of dreams,
So various, so beautiful, so new,
Hath really neither joy, nor love, nor light,
Nor certitude, nor peace, nor help for pain;
And we are here as on a darkling plain
Swept with confused alarms of struggle and flight,
Where ignorant armies clash by night.

(Matthew Arnold, *Poetry and Prose,* ed. J. Bryson [London, 1967], pp. 144–5)

The Night Battle

Half the controversies in the world are verbal ones; and could they be brought to a plain issue, they would be brought to a prompt termination. Parties engaged in them would then perceive, either that in substance they agreed together, or that their difference was one of first principles. This is the great object to be aimed at in the present age, though confessedly a very arduous one. We need not dispute, we need not prove, – we need but define. At all events, let us, if we can, do this first of all; and then see who are left for us to dispute with, what is left for us to prove. Controversy, at least in this age, does not lie between the hosts of heaven, Michael and his Angels on the one side, and the powers of evil on the other; but it is a sort of night battle, where each fights for himself, and friend and foe stand together. When men understand each other's meaning, they see, for the most part, that controversy is either superfluous or hopeless.

(J. H. Newman, *Newman's University Sermons* [London, 1970], pp. 200–1)

For Jan
with love

PREFACE

On deciding to put together a collection of pieces, written at different times for different purposes, one encounters a temptation and undergoes a risk. The temptation is to tinker too much. A theologian would have to be intolerably smug not to be deeply conscious of the fact, as he looks over his work, that he might have said it better then. But to say it differently now would not necessarily be to improve it. The only alterations that I have made to these essays, therefore, have been made in the interests of clarity.

The risk is that a collection such as this will lack the unity necessary to make it useful, and readable, as a book. But I selected these particular pieces because, for all the variety of their themes and levels of treatment, they seemed to me to illustrate two enduring preoccupations: an attempt to grapple with problems arising from the *historical* character of Christian faith and theology, and a conviction that, far from surrendering its critical integrity and (relative) autonomy, Christian theological reflection only attains its own proper rigour and significance if it is continually borne in mind that such reflection is dependent upon, secondary to, Christian faith and practice. I have therefore concentrated on these two issues in the Introduction.

If the emphasis in these essays is on questions of method, this is partly because the confusion and uncertainty which many Christians experience today is perhaps less obviously the expression of a crisis of faith than of a crisis of culture: we are not sure how to go about the business of *connecting* our

Christianity with other aspects of our life and experience; we are not sure what would count, and on what grounds, as appropriate ways of giving linguistic and conceptual expression to our faith. And these are therefore essays, 'essais', attempts, contributions to a discussion. In a situation such as ours, there is an inherent implausibility in the idea that any one man – be he theologian, philosopher, economist or politician – can come up with 'answers', with solutions to our common problems.

I would like to express my gratitude to the editors of *Concilium*, the *Epworth Review*, the *Heythrop Journal*, the *Irish Theological Quarterly* and the *Month*, who first published those pieces which appear here; to John M. Todd, for his advice and encouragement; and, above all, to my wife, who first suggested the use of Matthew Arnold's poem, who constructed the index, and without whose patient and constructive criticism these essays would be even less satisfactory than they are.

Cambridge
December 1978   Nicholas Lash

INTRODUCTION

In what sense is Christianity a 'historical' religion? What is the relationship, within the structure of Christian faith and theology, of christological to theological considerations? What is the relationship of theological reflection to the practice of Christian faith? The essays in this collection exemplify one of a number of possible approaches to such questions. In this Introduction, therefore, I propose briefly to indicate something of the character of this approach by contrasting it with that associated with the work of Professor Maurice Wiles.[1]

'What', asks Professor Wiles, 'does this much quoted phrase "a historical religion" imply and why is the thing implied felt to be so vital to the Christian faith?'.[2] He points out that the 'much quoted phrase' is ambiguous. It may mean that 'we are not therefore free to do whatever we like with it';[3] we are bound by the character, or language or content of our Christian origins; we are tied to our past. Alternatively, it may mean that, as historical, Christianity is 'something that exists through time' in the sense that 'it is its existence as a historical entity prepared to adapt itself to changing circumstances that ensures its continuing life and vitality'.[4] He suggests that, in

1 Professor Wiles will, I hope, forgive me for taking him, here and in Chapter Seven, as my 'partner in dialogue'. I do so because his work, with its persuasive lucidity and conceptual concision, seems to me admirably to illustrate an approach to problems of Christian theology which neatly contrasts with that which I am recommending.

2 M. F. Wiles, 'In what Sense is Christianity a "Historical" Religion?', *Explorations in Theology, 4* (London, 1979), p. 53.

3 Loc. cit.

4 Ibid., p. 54.

the nineteenth century, the tension between these two approaches came to be experienced as a tension between 'the truth of the text and of the history', the process of change and adaptation: 'a choice had had to be made between them and that choice ... had fallen on the side of history'.[5]

In the way that he thus sets out the problem, Professor Wiles seems to suppose that we have to choose *either* some form of what has been called 'non-historical orthodoxy' (or, as he puts it in a most misleading sketch of the character and concerns of Barth's theology, 'a positivist view of revelation'[6]) *or* a thorough-going relativist liberalism which, in practice, simply gives up the quest for criteria of Christian identity, practical and theoretical, through time and change.

That may seem harsh and yet, elsewhere, he maintains that 'any theology that emerges out of a serious attention to the Christian tradition has a *prima facie* claim to be considered a Christian theology'.[7] What is meant by 'emerges out of'? What counts as 'serious' attention? I wholeheartedly endorse Wiles' insistence on the irreducible pluralism of Christian theology, but when the net is cast so wide as to exclude only those theologies that either ignore or treat frivolously the Christian tradition (and which thus *includes*, for example, Feuerbach's *Essence of Christianity*, much Muslim theology and the theologies of the exuberant variety of syncretistic sects that flourish in Africa and Latin America) the concept of Christian theology is surely being so broadly defined as to make it, in practice, vacuous.

I hope that it is sufficiently clear, from these essays, that I am as convinced as he is that 'non-historical orthodoxy' is no longer a live option.[8] If, however, I am unable to adopt the strategy which he recommends, this is at least partly because,

5 Ibid., p. 56.
6 Ibid., p. 61.
7 M. F. Wiles, 'The Criteria of Christian Theology', *Working Papers in Doctrine* (London, 1976), p. 192.
8 Cf. e.g. the discussion of 'continuity and discontinuity' in Chapter Two (pp. 34–40), and the brief historical sketch in Chapter Four (pp. 65–9).

unlike him, I would wish to maintain that Christianity is 'a historical religion' in *both* his senses of the phrase; that the tensions to which this twofold character of Christianity gives rise are constitutive of Christian theology's task and responsibility; and that Christian faith – and therefore Christian theology – are radically dependent upon particular historical events.[9] This is, perhaps, the heart of the matter.

According to Professor Wiles, at the 'heart' of 'what is essential to Christianity . . . is the conviction that there is a God of love who is the ultimate source of the world'.[10] He may be right but, in his own words, 'How does he know? . . . How is such a claim to be made? Can it be supported by argument or is it something one either sees to be so – or fails to see, as the case may be?'.[11] He addresses these questions to the person who maintains (as I would wish to maintain) that Christian forms of faith in God do indeed 'stand or fall by certain particular historical happenings in the past'.[12] But at least it is clear that I regard some of the centrally constitutive claims of Christian belief as, in principle, vulnerable to falsification.[13] It is not clear to me that Professor Wiles does regard his central 'conviction' as thus vulnerable. But, if it is not, then in what sense are the arguments which he would adduce in support of his position to be considered serious *theoretical* arguments at all? Neither Professor Wiles nor I underestimate, I think, the complexity of the problem of the verification and falsification of religious beliefs. But I have the uneasy suspicion that Professor Wiles seeks, as it were, a 'faith without risks', whereas I have been at pains, in these essays, to emphasize (following Newman) the 'risk-laden' character of Christian faith, as of all forms of practical human commitment – domestic, religious or political.[14]

9 Cf. Chapter Two (pp. 40–4).
10 Wiles, ' . . . a "Historical" Religion?', p. 61.
11 Ibid., pp. 59–60.
12 Ibid., p. 61.
13 Cf. Chapter Five.
14 Cf. e.g. Chapter Five (pp. 80–1).

'My claim, therefore', says Professor Wiles, 'is that there is
nothing intrinsically more secure in a knowledge of God which
claims to rest on "certain historical events" whose historicity
is regarded as essential' than in 'a knowledge of God which
claims to rest on a more general historical experience (including that to which scripture bears witness) but which does not
treat any particular events within that broad spectrum as
essential'.[15] Leaving on one side, for the moment, the problem
of 'security', I am bound to say not only that I regard as
profoundly unsatisfactory, and as incompatible with the pay-
ment of 'serious attention to the Christian tradition', an
account of the 'heart' of Christian belief which is thus declared
to be compatible with, for example, the non-existence of Jesus,
but also that I find the appeal to 'general historical experience' intolerably abstract.[16]

'There is', says Wiles, 'a difference between saying that
what is essential is faith in Jesus as the Christ and describing it
as faith in God through Jesus Christ. The former gives to the
historical event a more firmly entrenched position than the
latter.'[17]

Yes, indeed, but I am unhappy – for two reasons – with this
formulation of contrasting approaches to the problem of the
relationship, within a Christian theology, of christological to
theological considerations. In the first place, I am not at all
clear that the latter approach, as employed by Wiles, can
properly be described as an approach to God *through* Jesus
Christ. In the second place, I am as conscious as he is of the
*theo*logical inadequacy of some accounts of Christian faith as
'faith in Jesus as the Christ'. However, laying these scruples

15 Wiles, art. cit., p. 63. His position here would seem to be similar to Van
    Harvey's, which I discuss in Chapter Three (pp. 50–1).
16 Cf. my criticisms of a similar abstractness in Küng (Chapter Eight, p.
    125) and my discussion of Professor Wiles' attempts to evacuate histori-
    cal particulars of significance, in Chapter Seven (pp. 115–7). In referr-
    ing to those theologians for whom God's action is 'not to be especially
    discerned in particular events at all' (Chapter Ten, p. 153), I have
    Professor Wiles, amongst others, in mind.
17 Wiles, art. cit., p. 60.

on one side, it seems evident that he takes the latter option, whereas I would take the former.[18]

It is worth insisting, however, that, in so doing, I am not suggesting that the 'starting point' of Christian theology is to be sought in christological rather than in theological considerations. I agree with Professor Wiles that 'Any claim that there is one and only one proper starting point for theology is evidence that the proponent of the claim has not yet grasped how theology has to be done'.[19] There are at least two reasons why this is so.

Firstly, the image of a 'starting point' for theological enquiry misleadingly suggests that theological argument is 'linear' in character. This is true, of course, in a trivial sense: namely, that conclusions follow from premises. Nevertheless, not only is the structure of argument, in almost any area of enquiry, considerably more complex than is apparent from a consideration of its small-scale formal features,[20] but the structure of argument in 'concrete matters' – in literary criticism, for example, or in historical and theological enquiry – is almost invariably 'cumulative' in character, as Newman was never tired of insisting.[21]

This is not to deny, of course, that some topics of Christian theology are more central than others, and that the more 'peripheral' topics presuppose and depend upon, or are asymmetrically related to, the more fundamental issues. Thus, for example, the question of the reality of God, and of the accessibility of the mystery of God to human experience and reflection, is – both in practice and in theory – fundamen-

18. Cf. e.g. Chapter One (p. 18); Chapter Two (p. 28 – but I hope that the whole of this second essay shows that I am as conscious as is Professor Wiles of the difficulty of appropriately *specifying* the 'essence' of Christianity).

19 M. F. Wiles, *The Remaking of Christian Doctrine* (London, 1974), p. 41.

20 Cf. S. Toulmin, *The Uses of Argument* (Cambridge, 1958) and the application of Toulmin's analysis to consideration of patterns of theological argument in D. Kelsey, *The Uses of Scripture in Recent Theology* (London, 1975).

21 Cf. my Introduction to J. H. Newman, *An Essay in Aid of a Grammar of Assent* (London and Notre Dame, 1979).

tal and (in this sense) 'prior' to any other theological question.[22] But both Karl Barth and Maurice Wiles would (I
imagine) accept that claim – a fact which should alone be
sufficient indication that to assert that the question of God is,
in this sense, the 'first' question in theology, is not to commit
oneself to either of the strategies outlined by Wiles. The differences between Barth and Wiles would, however, soon become
apparent if one asked them both: 'What is the relationship
between Christian faith and its theological reflection?' The
second reason why I find discussion of theology's 'starting
point' unprofitable is that such discussion tends to obscure the
difference between questions concerning the grounds of faith
and questions concerning the 'order' in which theological
topics might be treated.

Where the former issue is concerned, I should wish to argue
that specifically Christian faith, specifically Christian hope, is
generated by the historically, socially transmitted conviction
that it is in Jesus, in his life, teaching and fate, that God is
uniquely and definitively known as the God who saves: the
God who acts and will act to set his people free.[23] Any such
assertion makes Professor Wiles uneasy. But the grounds of
his unease seem to derive from an unsatisfactory view of the
character of Christian belief and its relationship to theological
reflection. Thus, for example, he suggests that someone who
claims that Christian forms of faith in God 'stand or fall by
certain particular historical happenings in the past'[24] would
be likely to support such a claim by arguing that 'Unless it has
been embodied in history in that way, then your faith is an
insufficiently grounded hypothesis'.[25]

But to speak of 'faith' as an 'hypothesis' – whether
sufficiently or insufficiently grounded – is to suppose that faith

22 Cf. my discussion of the three necessary conditions for a critical theo-
     logy, in Chapter One.
23 Cf. Chapter Three (pp. 49–50); Chapter Seven (pp. 113, 117); Chapter
     Nine.
24 Wiles, ' . . . a "Historical" Religion?', p. 61.
25 Loc. cit.

is some form of assent to propositions. This is to take a most misleadingly *theoretical* view of faith as a judgement or set of judgements arrived at on the basis of certain historical or metaphysical arguments.[26] This is a view of faith dear to rationalist apologists such as Paley; and it implies a view of the relationship between 'faith' and 'reason' which Newman, throughout his life, from the *University Sermons* to the *Grammar of Assent*, set himself to demolish.[27]

Patterns of responsible human action – in the love of husband and wife, in scientific research, in economic and political commitment and behaviour – imply and entail beliefs concerning what is the case. 'Blind' commitments, patterns of behaviour whose agents refuse to reflect upon and consider the arguments for and against their position, are suspect of illusion, fanaticism and irrationality. But it simply is not true that, before a pattern of action is to be judged 'reasonable', each individual participant in such action must have personally 'demonstrated' – historically or philosophically – that the beliefs implied by his actions are thus theoretically secured. The commitment of marriage may be expressible in the form: 'I believe that she loves me and that I love her.' But it would be extremely odd to describe that belief as a more or less adequately grounded 'hypothesis'. From one point of view it is indeed just that: hence the risk-laden character of all practical human commitments. But thus to characterize it – as if nobody should get married until they had *theoretically* 'proved' the presence of such reciprocal love – would be to give a very queer account of personal relationships (and something similar could be said of the rational component and implications

---

26 Similarly, at the end of his paper, Wiles says of the approach that he advocates that 'It makes it more likely that in making our faith judgements we will be making them on the basis of the best evidence available' (art. cit., p. 65). Cf. my discussion of Peter Baelz, in Chapter Five (pp. 82–3).

27 For some brief remarks on this, cf. Chapter One (pp. 14–5); Chapter Three (pp. 51–3); Chapter Six.

of, for example, patterns of social and political engagement and commitment).

Professor Wiles does indeed, in one place, rather reluctantly admit that 'there is a sense in which theology is parasitic upon the practice of religion'.[28] But, whereas this concession does not lead him to abandon that commitment to the primacy of the theoretical which pervasively characterizes his view of the relationship of theology to faith, I have sought, throughout these essays, to insist upon the primacy of practice.[29]

Is Christian believing fundamentally a matter of holding, theoretically, certain convictions which have implications for action and conduct? Or is it fundamentally a 'way of life', a form of practical engagement, with theoretical implications? If, with Professor Wiles, one takes the former view, then our beliefs will be judged 'securely' held in the measure that the patterns of historical and philosophical argument to which they stand as 'conclusions' are appropriately rigorous. If, as I have done in these essays, one takes the latter view, then the 'safeguards' of faith are rather to be sought in fidelity, in love, in the purity of action. Hence the analogies that are to be drawn between our growth in the knowledge of God and our growth in the knowledge of human persons; hence the convergence towards identity of faith and prayer.[30] And, as I have tried to show, it certainly does not follow from such a view of faith and its relationship to theological reflection, that the quality of that reflection – in historical, theological or philosophical enquiry – does not matter, any more than it would follow, from a commitment to the primacy of the practical in other areas (domestic or political, for example) that

28 'The Criteria of Christian Theology', p. 187. It is, I think, clear from the context in which Wiles makes that admission that we agree it to be a mistake to assume that, considered as types of discourse, the languages of religion and theology should be 'similar': cf. Chapter One (p. 15).

29 Cf. e.g. Chapter One (pp. 14–5); Chapter Two (pp. 43–4); Chapter Three (pp. 51–3); Chapter Four (pp. 72–4); Chapter Six (pp. 95–8); Chapter Nine (pp. 147–8); Chapter Ten (pp. 160–3).

30 On all these points, cf. the passages indicated in the previous note.

the work of psychologists, economists, sociologists and political theorists was of little account.

Professor Wiles' principal 'adversary', in the paper on
which I have been commenting, seems to be the proponent of
that form of (ultimately) rationalist, non-historical positivism
which characterizes certain kinds of Christian fundamental-
ism (both biblical and dogmatic). The alternative which he
proposes is certainly not fundamentalist, but it is similarly
rationalistic. As such, not only is it equally exposed to criticism from the sociologist (and, especially, from the sociologist
of knowledge) but it tends, as does the strategy of fundamen-
talism, to reduce theology to apologetics. Thus, for example,
in a passage to which I have already referred, Maurice Wiles
insists that 'there is nothing intrinsically more *secure* in a
knowledge of God which claims to rest on "certain historical
events"', than in 'a knowledge of God which claims to rest on
a more general historical experience ... but which does not
treat any particular events within that broad spectrum as
essential'.[31] But is it in quest of *security* that Christian faith and
theology are irresistibly drawn to the fact of a life and death
whose perceived significance disturbs our certainties, questions our values, and which – if it consoles and gives joy – does
so in so strange a manner as to deprive us of all claimed
possession of certainty, consolation and joy? To suppose that it
is the function of theological enquiry to give us 'security' in
our believing is to allow the preoccupations of apologetic to
distract theology from its proper tasks, to risk trivializing its
dangerous responsibility.

31 Wiles, ' ... a "Historical" Religion?', p. 63, my stress.

PART ONE

1. DOING THEOLOGY ON DOVER BEACH[1]

Members of ancient institutions are apt to bolster their fragile self-esteem by surrounding the offices of such institutions with an aura of portentousness. In this enterprise of legitimation robes, rituals and, perhaps especially, titles play no small part. Without such titles, the biographers of ecclesiastical, political and academic worthies might sometimes find it more difficult to convey the impression that the subjects of their study were, indeed, 'men of quality'. I am sharing with you something of the frame of mind in which, in starting to prepare this lecture, I returned to the work of my predecessors in the Norris-Hulse chair,[2] not out of any ungenerous spirit of denigration, but in the slightly desperate hope that a little healthy disrespect might enable me to see my own election as less implausible. And, of course, it didn't work. The exercise merely confirmed my conviction that these were men who had no need of the garnishings of office; that, very differently in each case, impressive intellectual and scholarly resources had been deployed by men of unusually powerful integrity. (Historical experience is, of course, more eclectic than historians of ideas sometimes allow: a letter from my uncle, Bishop Lash, suggested that Mrs Burkitt's imposing appearance remained a

1 An Inaugural Lecture delivered in the University of Cambridge in November 1978.
2 The Norrisian and Hulsean chairs were amalgamated in 1934. F. C. Burkitt, who had been Norrisian Professor from 1905–34, was Norris-Hulse Professor, 1934–35; C. H. Dodd, 1935–49; H. H. Farmer, 1949–60; D. M. MacKinnon, 1960–78.

more vivid impression than the details of her husband's scholarship. Bishop Lash, like his father, is an Emmanuel man. But whereas the bishop was a student at Westcott, my grandfather had been at Ridley; my family has always attempted a certain ecumenical generosity.)

Where my immediate predecessor was concerned I knew, of course, from the start, that demythologisation was futile. How could I not, having, for ten years now, derived incalculable benefit from his company? Not only from exposure to his quite unusual range of learning but, more fundamentally, from that passionate preoccupation with the significance of the particular which engages him in watchful war against the evasiveness of facile generalisation. Professor Owen Chadwick, in the lecture which he gave, in 1971, to mark the centenary of our Tripos, spoke of a shift of mood in Cambridge theology in the late 1930s. At that time, he said, 'the agonies and passions of mankind started to enter and complicate the philosophies'.[3] That Christian theology discovers and maintains its peculiar *akribeia* only in the measure that philosophy is thus 'complicated' by agony is, I think, amongst the more important lessons that Donald MacKinnon has helped me to learn.

In his inaugural lecture, he characterized the philosopher of religion as one set to work on 'the borderlands of theology'. 'In this territory', he said, 'concerned never to shirk the detailed exploration of the most varied manifestations of religion . . . the philosopher of religion today knows that his task is primarily critical'.[4] The lecture ended with a reference to those other 'men of the borderlands' who, like the philosopher of religion, 'make protesting raids upon the theologians' cherished homeland'.[5] That reference tantalizes: where, in a university setting, might such a theological 'homeland' be found, and how might the task of its inhabitants be appro-

---

3   W. O. Chadwick, 'The Cambridge Schools of Divinity'. I am grateful to Professor Chadwick for permission to quote from this lecture.

4   D. M. MacKinnon, *Borderlands of Theology and other Essays* (London, 1968), p. 41.

5   Ibid., p. 54.

priately specified? My intention is to offer some reflections on these two questions.

In an address delivered to the Christian Student Movement in October 1918, Baron Friedrich von Hügel (whose brother Anatole, Curator of the Museum of Ethnology and Archaeology, played an influential part in the establishment of St Edmund's House) asked: 'How then are we, scholars or scientists, to work or to develop our extant or incipient Churchmanship in the borderlands and mixed territories created for us by the very fact of our earnest scholarship and fervent Churchmanship?'.[6] If, on this account, we take the 'homeland' of theology to be the 'household of the faith', it would nevertheless appear to be the case that the Christian scholar possesses dual nationality and, by that very fact, to be unable anywhere to find himself simply 'at home'. My first suggestion, then, would be that it is today incumbent upon the theologian, also, to acknowledge that his task is 'primarily critical'. The sea has retreated too far down Dover beach for it to be otherwise.[7]

But to whom do I refer when I speak of 'the theologian', and how is his task to be differentiated from, and related to, the tasks of the textual critic, the exegete, the historian and the philosopher of religion? Or, to put it another way: what other enterprises, if any, should be fostered in a faculty such as ours, over and above those textual, exegetical and historical studies which have been its glory and which must, surely, continue to be among its principal strengths?

Studies of theological method often tackle such questions under the general rubric of the relationship between 'the study of theology' and 'the scientific study of religion'. This frame of reference, however, abstracting as it does from consideration

6 F. von Hügel, *Essays and Addresses on the Philosophy of Religion (First Series)* (London, 1921), p. 266.
7 There is internal evidence that, in the closing lines of 'Dover Beach', Matthew Arnold was drawing upon the image of the 'night battle' in the last paragraph of Newman's sermon on 'Faith and Reason, Contrasted as Habits of Mind' (the tenth of his *University Sermons*).

of that social context in which the work of the university is set, is dangerously narrow. In order to broaden it somewhat, we could perhaps adapt Max Weber's distinction between 'social science' and 'social policy' and ask: what of the relationships between the academic study of religion (in all its forms) and the policies of religious groups? It needs to be borne in mind that the establishment of such a distinction in practice and its clarification in theory are, and remain, tasks rather than achievements. To suppose that this distinction had been finally established or definitively clarified would be to have relaxed the constitutive tension between practice and theory on which the health of both theory and practice depend. It has been said of Weber that his 'greatness lies' in the extent to which, 'Both in his thought and in his life [he sought] to bear without flinching the enormous tension between detachment and engagement'.[8] That tension, and the conflicts which it generates, are fundamental to the quest.

These remarks may seem excessively skeletal. To put some flesh on them, let me recast the question: What of the relationships between the academic study of Christian origins (for example) and the work of preaching and of establishing programmes of pastoral care? Much twentieth-century English theological education seems to have proceeded on the assumption that the interactions between past and present forms of conduct and speech were not such as to demand critical, theoretical reflection. It was assumed, for example, that if a man had studied, with becoming 'objectivity', the Scriptures and the history and doctrine of the early Church, he was thereby appropriately equipped (so far as the academic dimension of his training was concerned) to function as preacher and pastor. Such assumptions are being rapidly eroded in practice. To expose them to more sustained theoretical examination than we have so far succeeded in doing might illuminate some features of our present theological discontent. (In taking preaching and pastoral care as analogous to the

8 P. L. Berger, *Pyramids of Sacrifice: Political Ethics and Social Change* (London, 1976), p. 255.

execution of Weberian social policy, I intend merely to reflect
the fact that, for much of this century, a high proportion of the
students in the Faculty were candidates for ordination. Today,
the terms of the analogy would be far more varied.)

What was it, however, that sustained the assumption that
the relationships between the academic study of Christian
origins and the practice of Christianity were not such as to
demand mediation at the theoretical as well as at the practical
level? Very tentatively, I would point to two related factors.
On the one hand, our historical studies and, especially, our
notions of historical objectivity, were infected by a positivism
the roots of which can be traced back to the seventeenth and
eighteenth centuries: we were untroubled by problems of
'hermeneutic' or the sociology of knowledge (especially our
own knowledge); we tended too easily to assume that the presuppositions and prior commitments of the student of history
no longer posed significant *theoretical* problems. On the other
hand, this element of positivism in our academic practice
enabled us to proceed as if the relationship between Christian
scholarship and Christian living bore at least a 'family
resemblance' to the relationship between, for example,
scientific research and its technological application. The task
of the preacher was to put into practice what he had learned in
the university: Christianity as the technology of theology!
(Incidentally, such a view of the relationship between scholarship and Christian living ascribed to the scholar a quite
unwarranted position of authority in the community of believers. But I shall return to this.)

In the story so far, no mention has been made of the
philosopher of religion. Where has he fitted in? The answer is
that quite often he has not: his work has been regarded as at
best a luxury, at worst (to adapt Professor MacKinnon's
image) a disruptive force, raiding the theologians' cherished
homeland. If, however, he succeeds in making himself indispensable, this will be partly a tribute to the quality of his
work, and partly an effect of the dawning recognition that the
interactions between historical scholarship and Christian liv-

ing do demand some form of critical, reflective mediation. I sometimes think that the widespread complaints about the 'gap' between pew or pulpit, on the one hand, and the effusions of academic rostra, on the other, are signals of this dawning recognition. So too, perhaps, is a deepening appreciation of the pervasiveness of problems of authority: the intractability of the quest for criteria of appropriate forms of action and speech.

But can this demand for some form of critical, reflective mediation be met by philosophy of religion alone? I believe not. Both the philosopher of religion and the theologian are concerned 'with religious practice in its vast complexity articulated in language'.[9] Both are concerned with issues not only of intelligibility and coherence, but also of truth. Both of them, unless they fall victim to that dilettantism, that counterfeit disinterestedness, satirised by Blondel as the style of those who maintain with the agility of a clown the inertia of a corpse,[10] experience within the texture of their exploration that tension between 'engagement' and 'detachment' by which Max Weber set such store. Nevertheless, if we reflect on the grounds of their engagement and the manner of their detachment the differences begin to appear.

If one sees the relationship between 'religion' and 'theology' in terms similar to those explored by Newman in the *Grammar of Assent*, then the engagement of the theologian has its ground in 'real assent' to that of which the language of religion seeks to speak. This may be true, but is not necessarily true, of the philosopher of religion. It is possible, as Pannenberg puts it, 'for philosophical enquiry to postpone the question of God, and even to avoid it if it refuses to formulate the question of reality as a whole'.[11] There are, perhaps, good philosophical reasons for refusing to formulate the question of reality as a whole. In which case the philosopher may, without loss of

9 MacKinnon, *Borderlands*, p. 52.
10 Cf. M. Blondel, *L'Action (1893)* (Paris, 1973), p. 9.
11 W. Pannenberg, *Theology and the Philosophy of Science* (London, 1976), p. 304.

integrity, continue to postpone the question. The theologian, however, as one whose enterprise is, formally and explicitly, an aspect of faith's quest for understanding, is constrained to attempt the impossible.

It must be insisted that I am trying to draw a distinction, not between groups of people, but between types of intellectual enterprise, between disciplines. The distinction is not, therefore, undermined by the fact, to which Professor MacKinnon's essay on 'Philosophy of Religion and Christology' bears witness,[12] that a philosopher who is himself a Christian may, in his own practice, unify the two enterprises. In such a case the two will, in Bernard Lonergan's phrase, acquire a 'performative unity'.[13] But would it not then be simpler to abolish the distinction, and merely to draw attention to the fact that the character of philosophical enquiry will be subtly influenced by the extent to which an individual practitioner does or does not seek to stand within the 'household of the faith'? This is an attractive suggestion, but I would nevertheless wish to argue that there are good reasons, partly historical and partly methodological (some of which will, I hope, become a little clearer later in this lecture) for continuing to draw a formal distinction between the two enterprises and, therefore, for suggesting that the demand for theoretical reflection on the relationships between scholarship and prayer, study and preaching, historical enquiry and Christian witness, cannot adequately be met by the philosophy of religion alone.

At this point – in order to widen the argument a little – I would like to suggest two further factors, the convergence of which renders at once urgent and more intractable the problem of such theoretical mediation. In the first place, the field of Christian studies has broadened remarkably in recent decades. And this broadening has taken two forms. On the one hand, it has been increasingly felt that for Christian theology to reflect more or less exclusively the history of Jewish

12 Cf. MacKinnon, *Borderlands*, pp. 55–81.
13 B. J. F. Lonergan, *Philosophy of God, and Theology* (London, 1973), p. 40.

and Christian religion, and of Western culture, is to condemn it to a parochialism which is inconsistent with its own universalistic thrust. Hence the pressure to find space for the study of Hinduism, Buddhism, Marxism and so on, in faculties of Christian studies. On the other hand, increasing emphasis has been laid on the indispensability of what George Lindbeck has called 'the study of religion as a generic reality'[14] from sociological, anthropological and psychological perspectives. This twofold broadening is undoubtedly desirable in principle. The extent to which, in practice, it is likely to impoverish rather than to enrich, is not my concern in this lecture. I would, however, just mention in passing the disquiet expressed in a recent report, of which Professor Lindbeck was the principal author, concerning the tendency, in American departments of religion, for 'generic' religious studies to acquire a predominant position. 'It is', he says, 'as if the study of language in general had engulfed the study of particular languages, of English, French or Chinese.'[15]

The point to which I wish to draw your attention, however, is this: when the field of study was restricted, in the way that it was, to one particular set of religious traditions, fundamental questions of value and significance were often hidden from view by that very restriction; however, the broadening of the field in the ways that I have indicated has now exposed these questions as ineluctably problematic.

In the second place, it is becoming increasingly doubtful whether a place should be found, in a modern university, for modes of theological enquiry that are not formally concerned with their own critical grounding. For the sake of clarity, let me oversimplify the matter by distinguishing between aspects of human existence; their more or less spontaneous expression in symbolic, linguistic and institutional forms; and the attempt theoretically or critically to reflect such expressions. Thus, for example, human existence finds expression in art,

14 G. A. Lindbeck, 'Theological Education in North America', *Bulletin of the Council on the Study of Religion*, viii, 4 (1977), p. 87.
15 Loc. cit.

social organisation, personal relations and languages of belief. Poetry, political action, the love of husband and wife, the articulation of faith in worship, preaching, suffering and symbolic self-expressions of communal belief: these things are more fundamental than their pale reflection in literary criticism, political theory, sciences of human relationship and academic theology. Nevertheless, it is for such reflection that universities immediately exist.

According to Professor Ninian Smart, 'Doing theology, in the proper sense, is articulating a faith'.[16] That description fails to differentiate between the more or less spontaneous expression of faith in liturgical, homiletic or theological discourse and attempts critically to reflect such expressions. To describe theology as the 'articulation of faith' is to acknowledge that, along with the 'languages' of law, politics and art, it is one of several 'ideological forms' in which social existence finds expression.[17] I accept Althusser's insistence, drawing on one strand in Marx's thought, that social existence without ideology is impossible: 'human societies secrete ideology as the very element and atmosphere indispensable to their historical respiration and life'.[18] But surely, except in a totalitarian society, the function of a university today is not the generation of such forms, but rather their critical assessment? As a result of his failure to differentiate between what we might call 'spontaneous' and 'critical' theological enquiry, the grounds on which Professor Smart allocates a place (albeit a very modest one) to the theologian in a faculty of religious studies are not lacking in ambiguity.[19] There is a similar ambiguity in Profes-

16 N. Smart, *The Science of Religion and the Sociology of Knowledge* (Princeton, 1973), pp. 6–7.
17 Cf. K. Marx, *Early Writings* (London, Penguin Books, 1975), p. 426.
18 L. Althusser, *For Marx* (London, 1977), p. 232.
19 Cf. Smart, *The Science of Religion*, p. 42. Gordon Kaufman's balanced and perceptive account of the relationship between 'theological' and 'religious' studies (cf. G. D. Kaufman, *God the Problem*, (Cambridge, Massachusetts, 1972), pp. 17–37), although more satisfactory than Smart's, similarly fails to come to grips with the problem of whether, and in what sense, theological inquiry can be critically grounded.

sor Lindbeck's account. Lindbeck describes 'theological education', as distinct from 'religious studies', as 'the intellectually responsible academic transmission and development of particular religious traditions'.[20] A lot depends upon what are to be counted as the constituents of intellectual responsibility.

Our problem is that of the relationship between 'theology' and the 'scientific study of religion'. I have so far tried to suggest some reasons for supposing that there should be a place, amongst the enterprises that are pursued in a faculty of theology and religious studies (a faculty the centre of whose concerns is, for historical and cultural reasons, primarily Christian) for a discipline whose principal function it is to attempt to give theoretical, critical expression to the interactions between 'science' and 'policy', between scholarship and strategies of Christian living. In so far as the concept of 'theology' is taken, very generally, to refer to the 'articulation of faith', we might describe the discipline for the desirability of whose presence I have been arguing as 'critical theology'. Since, however, all labels are not only inadequate but liable to mislead, a few comments on that description are in order.

In the first place, the enterprise of critical theology, as I would wish to characterize it, would clearly inherit many of the tasks usually associated with both 'fundamental' and 'systematic' theology. But the concept of 'fundamental' theology is notoriously ambiguous, and the concept of 'system', with its seductive, promethean overtones of panoramic organisation, allows the theologian too easily to lose sight of the fact that his work, like that of the philosopher, is irreducibly interrogative in character.

In the second place, in speaking of 'critical' theology (and it is clear that, in doing so, I am using the notion in a somewhat different sense from that which Professor Charles Davis gave to it in last year's Hulsean lectures) I have in mind what Professor MacKinnon has described as the 'censorial' task of the theologian.[21] As Karl Barth put it: the 'scientific' quality

20 Lindbeck, 'Theological Education', p. 85.
21 Cf. MacKinnon, *Borderlands*, p. 41.

of theology 'consists not so much in confirming as rather in disturbing Church proclamation as it meets it in its concrete forms to date, and above all in the present concrete forms of the day'.[22]

In the third place, however, I am aware of the fact that to speak of theology as 'critical' may give the impression that I am underestimating the constructive or creative responsibilities of the theologian. That is not my intention. Literary 'criticism' is, I take it, a constructive enterprise, but its creativity is constrained by the first-order levels of language and symbolisation with which it engages.

I have been arguing for the desirability of an enterprise that I have described as that of 'critical theology'. It is, however, one thing to urge the desirability of some particular undertaking. It is quite another matter to specify the conditions of its possibility. What I propose to do, therefore, in what remains of this lecture, is to indicate what seem to me to be the necessary conditions for the execution of the enterprise of critical theology, of that mode of reflection which seeks critically to articulate religious and, specifically, Christian faith.

The inability of critical theology to postpone the question of God arises from the fact that such theology is a particular form of faith's quest for understanding. Restricting my attention to Christian theology, I would wish to argue (although, within the limits of a lecture whose scope is already sufficiently over-ambitious, assertion must stand substitute for argument) that Christian faith is illusory, Christian hope unfounded, if there is not that to which, as their transcendent ground and goal, such faith and hope refer. In other words, if a reductionist sociological analysis of the referent or referents of the concept of God were correct (whether the form of that analysis be Feuerbach's, or Durkheim's, or anybody else's) then Christian faith is illusory and Christian hope unfounded. It would follow that critical theology, understood as operating within the movement of faith – albeit as an operation which, within that

22 K. Barth, *Church Dogmatics*, *I/1* (Edinburgh, 1936), p. 323.

movement, sought the painful purification of critical detachment – would be deprived of its object. It would be possible
learnedly to record other men's uses of the concept of God, or
painstakingly to analyse concepts of God and the logic of their
use, whether or not Feuerbach or Durkheim were correct. But
a discipline that seeks critically to reflect the spontaneity of
faith's response, a discipline that seeks reflectively to speak of
God, is deprived of all coherence and validity if there is not
that to which its discourse refers.

To put it very simply: alone amongst the types of enquiry
pursued in a faculty of theology and religious studies, critical
theology has as one of its necessary conditions that there is
God. I cannot emphasize too strongly that, from this conclusion, *nothing positive follows*. I have not said whether or not this
condition is fulfilled, or whether or in what manner it could be
known to be fulfilled. Even if it were fulfilled and known to be
fulfilled, nothing that I have yet said would entitle us to suppose the enterprise to be either possible or profitable. I have
only said that, if this condition is not fulfilled, then the discourse of critical theology is, in fact, as illusory as the faith it
purports critically to reflect. Before moving on, however, it
may be worth making two comments on the model of the
relationship between 'faith' and 'theology' presupposed by
this account.

In the first place, this model has evident affinities, as I
suggested earlier, with Newman's account, in the *Grammar of
Assent,* of the interdependence of 'religion' and 'theology', and
also with that view of the relationship between action and
reflection which leads Latin-American 'liberation theologians'
to speak of theology as 'critical reflection on Christian
praxis'.[23] According to Marx, an illusory belief in the autonomy of theoretical discourse is the besetting sin of 'bourgeois
idealism'. Of that sin, much contemporary English theology is
still guilty. I hinted at this earlier when I criticized our tendency to proceed as if the relationship between scholarship

---

23   G. Gutierrez, *A Theology of Liberation* (London, 1974), p. 13.

and Christian living bore a family resemblance to the relationship between scientific research and its technological application. I should perhaps add that, in opting for a more 'materialist' account of the relationship between theory and practice, action and reflection, it is not at all my intention to
encourage that pietistic anti-intellectualism which is sometimes offered as an alternative to a sterile and ultimately illusory rationalism. The supposition that, in religious matters, the
primacy of the practical dispenses us from the *ascesis* of
theoretical enquiry is often no more than evidence, either of
mindless fanaticism or, in Professor Herbert Farmer's phrase,
of 'that easy-going confidence in God's goodness which always
threatens Christian piety, especially when it is conjoined with
economic comfort and privilege'.[24]

In the second place, it is illegitimate to infer, from that close
interdependence of religious practice and theological
reflection which I am recommending, that the mode of
theological discourse should be identical with or similar to the
mode or modes of first-order religious discourse. Some such
inference is often drawn, partly from a commendable desire to
prevent preaching and theology from 'drifting too far apart',
and partly as a result of our native suspicion of abstraction. If,
however, I were to urge that the discourses of political practice
and political theory should be kept 'closely related', I would
be insisting on the need continually to submit theoretical
claims to the resistant complexity of the facts of social organisation; I would not necessarily be suggesting that, considered
as types of discourse, the language used in textbooks of political theory should be 'similar' to the language of the hustings.
The 'abstract' or 'impersonal' quality of political or theological theoretical discourse does not, *eo ipso*, render them inappropriate to their subject-matter.

I have suggested that it is a necessary condition for the
enterprise of critical theology that there is God. I have not
even begun to hint, however, at the difficulties that beset

24 H. H. Farmer, *The World and God* (London, 1936), p. 232.

attempts more precisely to specify this condition. There are various strategies for attempting to meet these difficulties. The first, and perhaps the least satisfactory (although it is still widely adopted) is to continue to speak about God 'as if', in Pannenberg's phrase, 'nothing had happened', [25] as if classical forms of theism had not been subjected to the most searching conceptual and moral criticism. The second is to proceed as if these difficulties could be met by repeating often enough that 'God is not an object', and by seeking to persuade oneself and one's hearers that concepts such as that of 'ultimate concern', or 'the beyond in our midst', or 'absolute mystery', or 'the power of the future', are easier to negotiate than 'Father' or 'supreme being'. The third-strategy is that of reticence. To take refuge in silence may, however, be an evasion of the responsibility to speak. 'After Auschwitz', says Adorno, 'there is no word tinged from on high, not even a theological one, that has any right unless it underwent a transformation.'[26] But he adds: 'Not even silence gets us out of the circle. In silence we simply use the state of objective truth to rationalize our subjective incapacity.'[27] Even if the appropriate answer to George Steiner's question: 'What is there to *say* about Belsen?'[28] is 'Nothing', it does not follow that such silence is appropriately embodied in learned commentaries on the Old Testament or in massive treatises on problems of theological method. Busily to evade the issue is still evasion.

With these remarks, however, I have begun to treat of topics more suitably discussed under the heading of the second necessary condition that I would propose for the enterprise of critical theology. Critical theology, I now want to suggest, is not possible unless (and the formulation is Pannenberg's) God is 'accessible ... by his own action'.[29] Once

25 W. Pannenberg, 'Types of Atheism and Their Theological Significance', *Basic Questions in Theology*, Vol. 2 (London, 1971), p. 189.
26 T. W. Adorno, *Negative Dialectics* (London, 1973), p. 367.
27 Loc. cit.
28 G. Steiner, *After Babel: Aspects of Language and Translation* (Oxford, 1975), p. 185.
29 Pannenberg, *Theology and the Philosophy of Science*, p. 310.

again, it is because this is a necessary condition of non-illusory faith that it is a necessary condition of theology. And, once again, very little follows positively from the specification of the condition.

If God is not accessible by his own action, accessible *in* human actions and thoughts, human deeds and words, then Christian faith, hope and obedience are merely the reaching out from slavery to unattainable freedom. Such reaching out may have its own tragic nobility. It may even, so long as it can be sustained, exercise a transformative influence in human affairs: it might well, in certain circumstances, function as stimulant and critique, rather than as narcotic. But, unless God is accessible by his own action, Christian faith expresses only man's hope, and theology is rendered incapable of speaking of God.

Even if, however, this second condition were to be met, it would not follow that critical theology was necessarily possible. Even if, for example, human experience, or certain features of human experience, were in fact experience of God's action, it would not necessarily follow that they were recognisable as experience of God's action. This is a favourite theme in the writings of Karl Rahner, who insists that 'the possibility of experiencing grace, and the possibility of experiencing grace *as* grace are not the same thing'.[30]

Moreover, even if God's accessibility by his own action were recognisable as such, the constraints imposed upon critical theology might turn out to be very narrow. It could be that the only resources available, in practice, for giving expression, in worship and preaching, to faith's response to God's action, were such as to be, not simply inadequate for their subject-matter (for this is inevitable) but actively and destructively misleading. In such situations, critical theology could only take the form of negative theology; possibly, indeed, of the very negation of theology. Such questions are not to be decided in the abstract, but by reflecting, in particular histori-

30 K. Rahner, 'Concerning the Relationship Between Nature and Grace', *Theological Investigations,* Vol. I (London, 1961), p. 300.

cal circumstances, on the linguistic and symbolic resources concretely available. The issue may become clearer if, at this point, I offer some tentative reflections on what, taking up an image I made use of a little earlier, we might describe as the christological character of Christian theology 'after Auschwitz'.

Is Christian faith such that it finds the ground of its hope for the future of man in its experience of that which it calls 'God', seeing in Jesus a privileged instantiation of this vision of man? Or is Christian faith such that it receives its hope for the future of man from the history of Jesus? In the former case, critical reflection on faith will, indeed, include a 'christological chapter', but it will be only that. In the latter case, christological considerations will shape and specify every move that we make in the attempt critically to reflect Christian faith and hope. In speaking of the 'christological character' of theology, I am simply making a plea for the serious consideration of the second of these two options, an option that is undoubtedly disturbing in its dependence upon historical particularity and which is, partly for this reason, somewhat unfashionable in English theology today.

A God whose presence and action does not continually call in question our conceptual and institutional achievements is a God who has been idolatrously 'domesticated', whether or not lip-service continues to be paid to his transcendence. Christian faith has too often sought the security of possession, of the domestication of the absolute, both practically and theoretically. And, in so far as it has done so, it has contributed to the enslavement of man, in the name of the authority and sovereignty of God. Few men have perceived this more acutely, or criticized it more savagely, than Nietzsche. But the savagery of his *moral* protest against Christianity is in striking contrast to the sensitivity of his characterisation of the one of whom he said: 'In reality there has been only one Christian, and he died on the Cross.'[31]

31   F. Nietzsche, 'The Anti-Christ', *Twilight of the Idols and the Anti-Christ* (London, Penguin Books, 1968), p. 151.

Whitehead, as far as I know, never made a close study of Nietzsche. But the person of Jesus, and the manner of his death, exercised a similar fascination. And when Whitehead remarked: 'I consider Christian theology to be one of the great disasters of the human race',[32] he was voicing a protest not unlike Nietzsche's: a protest against concepts of God, and of God's relationship with man, which had shown themselves to be, in practice (whatever the theory), incompatible with the freedom and flourishing of man. This question of the compatibility of the freedom of man with the sovereignty of God is still, as both a practical and a theoretical issue, the central question to which Christianity should address itself. Horkheimer gave this question classic expression when he remarked: 'the more Christianity brought God's rule into harmony with events in the world, the more the meaning of religion became perverted ... Christianity lost its function of expressing the ideal, to the extent that it became the bedfellow of the state'.[33]

It is only too easy to show that Nietzsche, Whitehead, Horkheimer and countless others have, in their treatment of Christian practice and theology, selectively misrepresented and distorted the traditions they purport to describe. But do not such (undoubtedly necessary) demonstrations of the inadequacy of the criticism too often evade, rather than meet, its fundamental challenge? And if, at the level of Christian faith and practice, that challenge can only be met by a form of Christianity which is, in *fact*, contributory to man's freedom in history, how is it to be met at the level of theory, of Christian theology? One answer, of course, is the pietist one: we should seek to speak simply of Jesus, and eschew all abstract systematisation. But this answer is as unreal, and ultimately as irresponsible, as is the countercultural illusion that anarchy, the dissolution of institutions, is the road to effective liberation from oppressive social structures. Pietism is, in the last analysis, as evasive as Matthew Arnold's cry: 'Ah, love, let us

32 L. Price, *Dialogues of Alfred North Whitehead* (London, 1954), p. 171.
33 M. Horkheimer, *Critical Theory* (New York, 1972), p. 129.

be true To one another!'[34] Unstructured human existence, socially, linguistically, conceptually, is an autistic illusion. The quest is for ever less inappropriate structures. The problem therefore becomes: how is this quest to be pursued in the enterprise of *fides quaerens intellectum*, of faith's search for linguistic and conceptual expression?

I may seem, in the last few minutes, to have wandered from the point. But it was only a detour. The problem with which I began was that of how, using whatever linguistic and symbolic resources are concretely available, theology today might hope to give less than wholly inappropriate expression to Christian faith. I suggested that the christological character of Christian theology might provide a clue. We are now in a position to follow up that suggestion. It is a consequence of the christological character of Christian theology that the *hubris* of absolutisation by which, in its unavoidable quest for systematic and theoretical expression, such theology is ever threatened, is effectively disciplined by the radical contingency of that which gives both faith and theology their shape and specificity.

It follows, perhaps, that, if the theologian is to speak, not too misleadingly, of the ground and goal of Christian faith, he may need to see his task as having at least as much in common with that of the literary critic as with that of the metaphysician. Metaphysicians are perennially tempted to misconceive the generality of their concern as a licence for disengagement from the particular. And, at least in our time, when metaphysical enquiry is frequently misconceived, by friend and foe alike, as a form of freewheeling speculation, it would seem to be the poets and novelists, rather than the philosophers, who are best placed to communicate the universal significance of contingent particulars.

Auerbach said of Virginia Woolf that she 'put the emphasis on the random occurrence, to exploit it not in the service of planned continuity of action but in itself. And in the process something new and elemental appeared: nothing less than the

---

34   M. Arnold, 'Dover Beach'.

wealth of reality and depth of life in every moment to which we surrender ourselves without prejudice'.[35] Christian faith is ineluctably grounded in random occurrence. Its forms of first-order discourse are, accordingly, primarily narrative in character. Only by respecting the narrative or dramatic character of the languages of belief can theology hope to remains sufficiently sensitive to 'that sense of complexity, even paradox, which, in the public language of our poets, novelists and dramatists, is, in origin, theological'.[36]

I do not know whether, and in what circumstances, Christian theology can hope to take positive rather than negative form 'after Auschwitz'. This is at least as much a practical as a theoretical question. But we forget at our peril that that 'random occurrence' with which theological reflection is primarily concerned has more in common with the gas-chamber than with 'the moment in the rose-garden'.[37] This being the case, insistence on the christological character of Christian theology might at least help to preserve the theologian from indulging in 'the easy speeches that comfort cruel men',[38] and from slackening the paradox that counterpoints Christian joy with the recognition that the world that lies before us, on Dover beach, has neither 'certitude, nor peace, nor help from pain'.

I have suggested that the reality of God, and his accessibility 'by his own action', are necessary conditions for the enterprise of critical theology. In the last few minutes, I have begun to hint at a third such condition, on which my comments will be very brief. It is a necessary condition for the enterprise of Christian theology that there exist a community, or communities, whose action and speech are perceived, by their members, to give contingent expression to God's historical accession. Unless this third condition is met, there are no patterns of action and first-order speech which can be given

---

35 E. Auerbach, *Mimesis: The Representation of Reality in Western Literature* (Princeton, 1953), p. 552.
36 J. Coulson, 'Belief and Imagination', *Downside Review*, xc (1972), p. 14.
37 T. S. Eliot, 'Burnt Norton', line 85, *Four Quartets*.
38 From G. K. Chesterton's hymn, 'O God of Earth and Altar'.

critical, reflective expression in theology. Were this third condition not met, Christian theology would be at most an
interpretation of human history without enduring empirical
grounds and warrants; it could only speak of yesterday, and
never from today. Once again, this is only a necessary condition. It may well be the case, to repeat a point that I made
earlier, that, in particular concrete circumstances, the available resources of Christian action and speech are such that the
form of their critical reflection could only be negative. If there
is such a third necessary condition for the enterprise of Christian theology (and it may not have escaped your notice that my
three conditions run in parallel, as it were, to the three articles
of the creed) it follows that the vitality and concrete 'truthfulness' of Christian speech and action is a precondition of the
possibility of theology rather than (as seems often to be supposed) the other way round. And this should once again serve
as a reminder to the academic theologian that, even if his role
within the Christian community is indispensable, it is
nevertheless an exceedingly modest one.

I began this lecture by suggesting why it is that, as I see it,
some place should be found today, in a Christian faculty of
theology and religious studies, for a mode of theological
enquiry whose function it would be theoretically to reflect the
relationship between linguistic, exegetical, historical and
social scientific aspects of religious studies, and the formulation of policies of Christian speech and action, and why such a
discipline, although frequently indistinguishable in practice
from the philosophy of religion, would nevertheless be distinct
from it in principle. In the second half of the lecture I have
tried to specify the three necessary conditions for this enterprise of what I have called 'critical theology'.

It is not, I think, simply predictable academic caution that
has inhibited me from attempting the further task of specifying
the sufficient conditions for such an enterprise. It is, rather,
the conviction that, in so far as any such further specification
were to be possible at all within the limits of historical existence, its grammar would be closer to that of the language of

prayer than of theoretical argument. Perhaps, therefore, I might end with a prayer of St Thomas Aquinas, which I have chosen not simply to meet the conventional expectation that any Roman Catholic is likely to refer to Aquinas at some point in the discussion, but also because it was used by Professor C. H. Dodd to open each session of the panel of New Testament translators of the New English Bible. And you will perhaps forgive me if I quote it, as he used to do, in a forgotten tongue: 'Domine Deus ac Deus noster, qui vere fons luminis diceris, infundere dignere super animi nostri tenebras tuae radium claritatis, duplicas a nobis removens tenebras, peccati scilicet et ignorantiae, in qua nati sumus. Da nobis intelligendi acumen, interpretandi subtilitatem, eloquendi gratiam. Ingressus instituas, progressus dirigas, egressus compleas, per Jesum Christum Dominum nostrum.'[39]

39 F. W. Dillistone, *C. H. Dodd* (London, 1977), p. 205.

PART TWO:
PLURALISM AND DISCONTINUITY

The problem of Christianity's practical and theoretical quest for criteria of identity has many aspects. Thus, for example, that quest is sometimes formulated in terms of a quest for continuity across the manifest discontinuities of historical and cultural change. This is the angle from which the problem is approached in Chapter Two, where two of the issues discussed in the Introduction, namely, the sense in which Christianity is an 'historical' religion, and the relationship between faith and theological reflection, are shown to be closely connected.

The second of these two issues is also a central theme in Chapters Three and Five – although the treatment in the latter chapter is more informal, more 'personal', than that adopted in the former.

It is, today, impossible seriously to discuss questions concerning Christianity's quest for maintained identity without adverting to the problem of historical interpretation, of 'hermenuetics': how are we to discover the extent to which we can and do succeed in 'understanding' words spoken, actions performed, in cultural contexts significantly different from our own? Chapter Four indicates the 'state of play' in regard to such questions as they affect the work of the Christian theologian.

2. CONTINUITY AND DISCONTINUITY IN THE CHRISTIAN UNDERSTANDING OF GOD

The more I reflect on it, the more it seems to me that the topic suggested for this paper is vast, complex, intractable.[1] All that I shall attempt to do is to reflect on the terms in the title in the hope that, by so doing, I may pick out some of the key issues and so provide myself with the materials out of which to construct, in the final section, a tentatively sketched personal response to the cluster of problems which the title suggests.

Christian *Understanding of God*
In the first place, our topic is continuity and discontinuity in the *Christian* understanding of God. I take it, therefore, that we may focus our reflection, not on problems of philosophical theology, or the comparative study of religion, but on problems of specifically Christian belief. Although I shall make some remarks from the standpoint of the psychology and sociology of religious belief and language, I intend to operate for the most part within the perspective of *fides quaerens intellectum*. That is to say, I shall presuppose and not argue for the legitimacy of Christian faith and Christian hope.

---

1 Originally delivered at a conference, at St Patrick's College, Maynooth, on 'The God of Christians in Today's World', and first published in the *Irish Theological Quarterly*, xliv (1977), pp. 291–302. Although some passages have been revised in the interests of clarity, its informal style still reflects the purpose, as introductory to a discussion, which it was originally intended to serve.

To say that our concern is with continuity and discontinuity in the *Christian* understanding of God is also to say that we must not lose sight of the christological dimension of the problem.

Here, speaking of 'continuity', one of the perennial concerns of Christian theological enquiry has been with the manner in which our knowledge of Christ affects, and is affected by, the inevitably agnostic quality of all human discourse concerning God (a theme on which I shall comment later on). Augustine, the Cappadocians, Aquinas, Schleiermacher, Barth, Rahner – these, and countless others, have been concerned with the problem of how it is possible coherently to insist, at one and the same time, on the radical transcendence, and hence incomprehensibility, of God, and on the fact that, in Christ, man may in some sense 'truly', in his living and thinking, enter into and 'apprehend' the mystery of God.

But the permanence, or continuity, of this concern, thus formally expressed, must not allow us to lose sight of the discontinuity, the incompatibility, that obtains between different ways of responding to that concern. Let me take just one instance of the sort of discontinuity between christological approaches that I have in mind, an instance which has, in many ways, dominated the history of modern theological thought.

If we may come to a 'true', and hence salvific, liberating, healing, understanding of God, quite independently of the fact of Christ; if the fact of Christ merely fills in certain details, confirms or adjusts certain features, of a concept of God at which we could arrive, and which we could know to be in some sense 'true', quite independently of Christ; then the christological dimension of our problem loses some of its urgency. If, on the other hand, the fact of Christ implicitly revolutionizes our understanding of God; if the fact of Christ makes possible a 'knowledge' of God which, as in some sense 'given', contrasts with those models of absolute mystery which human need and human hope construct and project, then the christological dimension retains all its urgency and indispensability.

And for us, who live in the latter part of the twentieth century, this creates a problem to which I shall later return. For us, the experience and understanding of God in Christ is ineluctably mediated by a network of historical, exegetical and hermeneutical considerations many of which seem in principle incapable of definitive resolution. It is as if a century and a half of historical consciousness had had the effect, not of bringing us into closer cognitive contact with our past, but rather of rendering that past *opaque*, unreadable. And must we not say that, in the measure that the face and voice of Jesus the Christ have been rendered invisible and inaudible by this 'opacity' of the historical, then our hope of hearing God's voice, of seeing his face (even if in a glass, darkly) has been fundamentally threatened?

Christian **Understanding** *of God*

In the second place, our concern is with continuity and discontinuity in the Christian *understanding* of God. I take this to mean, on the one hand, that our concern is not directly with the problem of continuity and discontinuity in the Christian *experience* of God (even though this may be, from the religious point of view, undoubtedly the more fundamental issue) but with the problem of continuity and discontinuity in the Christian attempt to articulate and interpret that experience linguistically, conceptually, symbolically. In thus distinguishing between 'experience' and the languages which shape and mediate that experience, I am not suggesting that there is, at least in the ordinary way, any such thing as pre-linguistic or non-linguistic human experience. I take it that all human experience – including, if there be such, experience of God – is, in some sense, linguistically structured. Even to say that much is to poke one's finger into a hornet's nest of philosophical problems. My concern, at the risk of being stung, is simply to register disquiet at the ease with which some theologians distinguish between 'religious experience' and the interpretation of such experience.

On the other hand, however, in so far as we are concerned with the problem of continuity and discontinuity in the Christian understanding of God, I take it that we are not directly concerned with the problem of continuity and discontinuity between Christian *statements* concerning God. In spite of the first Vatican Council's insistence that the permanence of dogma 'attaches to the meaning and not to the formula',[2] there is still a widespread tendency to assume that, if we *say* what was once said, we necessarily believe what was once believed and, conversely, that somebody who is reluctant today to employ ancient statements has departed from ancient understanding. Which begs the whole question of hermeneutics.

Where continuity is concerned, if I were asked to list those features of Christian discourse concerning God which have recurred most persistently in the course of the Church's history, in an impressive variety of social and cultural contexts, one which would come high on my list would be the conviction that it is impossible to understand God.

This conviction has its roots in our Jewish prehistory, and it finds expression, again and again, in patristic, medieval and renaissance theology and spirituality. It may not be the only thing which Christians have said, and felt impelled to say, concerning the mystery of God. But surely one of the most striking novelties of modern (that is to say, post-seventeenth century) Catholic theological and ecclesiastical discourse concerning God has been the subordination, sometimes almost the elimination, of that apophatic dimension which, for sixteen centuries, was so central a feature of the Christian understanding of God: the dimension which insists, whatever the price paid in the straining and bending of logic and coherence, that the God we know cannot be understood. It is already over a hundred years since Matthew Arnold protested, in *Literature*

2 B. J. F. Lonergan, *Method in Theology* (London, 1972), p. 323. Lonergan is commenting on the third canon to Chapter 4 of the Constitution *Dei Filius*.

and Dogma, against 'the licence of affirmation in our Western theology'.

In order to explain the profound shift which occurred in theological sensibility, at the time of the 'birth of the modern world', it would be necessary to examine, amongst other things, the influence of that positivist apologetic stance which became, and for so long remained, a dominant feature of modern Catholic consciousness. But the question that we have to ask ourselves is: can we sustain, and do we wish to sustain, this modern conviction that only knaves and fools find it difficult to speak of God with ease and assurance? Or do we find ourselves impelled to adopt a more ancient, and more dialectically structured stance, for which speech about God would, for faith, be as imperative as it is impossible? Perhaps only a faith that has lost its nerve feels obliged continually to insist that it is quite sure of itself, that it knows quite clearly what is to be said concerning the mystery of God.

This is by no means a merely theoretical issue. If the tone of our theological and ecclesiastical discourse were to become again more contemplatively unsure of *itself,* more the voice of prayer and hope, less cognitively and institutionally self-assertive, then we might find it more difficult than we have sometimes done in the recent past to speak glibly and uncomplicatedly about the 'will of God', the 'law of God', and so on. Immense human suffering has been caused by people who, lacking any very profound understanding of themselves, were nevertheless quite confident that they understood God.

Christian Understanding of **God**

In the third place, our concern is with continuity and discontinuity in the Christian understanding of *God.* Under this heading there is one basic problem, one widespread tendency in current theological writing, on which I wish briefly to comment, if only because any discussion of our topic that entirely failed to advert to it would be guilty of frivolity and cowardice.

This problem is the problem of truth. We are concerned, and rightly concerned, with the 'meaningfulness' and 'relevance', the concrete intelligibility and communicability, of theological statement. But this wholly admirable concern is sometimes so structured as to bypass the question of the truth of theological expression, or even to suggest that to raise this question is in some way inappropriate or improper.

To insist that the question of the truth of theological statements demands to be directly confronted is not to deny or to minimize the complexity of the question. Living, as we do, a long time after Feuerbach, quite a long time after Freud, and in an intellectual climate heavily impregnated with the achievements of the sociology of knowledge, we are not likely to overlook the fact that our models of God are 'projections' of our human hopes and fears; that they are produced by, reflect and symbolically express, visions of man and patterns of human organisation. But are religious and theological models simply, without remainder, 'projections' and social symbolizations? If they are, then we can indeed continue to discuss the 'truth' and 'falsity' of theological claims but we should at least have the honesty to admit that, in so doing, we are appealing to a notion of theological truth which is, in certain crucial respects, fundamentally discontinuous from that to which most of our Christian predecessors appealed.

There is, says Renford Bambrough, a difference between the assertion that Homer makes when he says that 'Poseidon is angry', and the assertion that we would be making if we uttered the same statement. 'One way of describing the difference would be to say that when Homer says that Poseidon is angry he is offering what is meant to be an *explanation* of the lashing of the waves, whereas when we say that Poseidon is angry we are giving no more than a picturesque *description* of the lashing of the waves.'[3]

Both Homer and ourselves say: 'Poseidon is angry.' Both of us would claim that, if the sea is stormy, then our assertion is

3 R. Bambrough, *Reason, Truth and God* (London, 1969), p. 30.

true. But the shift from Homer's description to ours does seem to have eliminated a central feature of Homer's assertion: namely, the claim that a non-empirically observable being, called Poseidon, causes the disturbance of the waves.

Bambrough's parable raises two sets of questions discussion of which lies outside the scope of this essay. In the first place, the point of the parable holds even if it is maintained, as I should wish to maintain, that questions concerning the reality of God are not appropriately articulated in terms of the existence or non-existence of a 'non-empirically observable being'. In the second place, there are questions concerning the role of philosophical enquiry in assessing theological truth-claims. To put the matter very simply: I do not regard it as the business of philosophical theology to attempt directly to settle questions concerning the truth or falsehood of theological claims. Philosophers should, it seems to me, stick to the more modest task of scrutinizing the intelligibility, the formal coherence or incoherence, of theological argument. Because I recognize that philosophy has this task, I cannot be convicted of 'fideism', although I would wish to maintain that, in the ontological, even if not necessarily in the epistemological order, perception of the truth of theological claims is the fruit, not the precondition, of the response of faith to God's initiating love.

What I am concerned to urge, however, is that, if someone wishes to opt for a resolutely reductionist account of the truth-conditions of theological statement, an account which would eliminate the necessity of any reference to a God who is not reducible to society or history, time or the cosmos, then he should openly acknowledge the fact that he is opting for a fundamental break in the history of the Christian understanding of God. There are, undoubtedly, a whole range of 'theisms' which are simply no longer available as serious intellectual options, but I still wish to affirm – perhaps better, confess – the transcendent reality of the God of Christian hope. To paraphrase a famous protest of Karl Barth's: 'You cannot speak of Poseidon by speaking of the sea in a loud voice.'

Continuity and Discontinuity

So far, I have simply tried to indicate something of the range of problems with which any attempt to speak to the title of this paper should be concerned. Next, I propose to attend more directly to the first two words in the title: *continuity* and *discontinuity* in the Christian understanding of God.

I take it that, as Christians, we are concerned faithfully to hear, and obediently to respond, in deed and word, to the God whom we confess to have definitively expressed himself in the person, words, work and fate of Jesus of Nazareth.

It is widely assumed that, because that is our concern, therefore discontinuity in the Christian understanding of God poses a threat, and continuity is at once God's promise and our responsibility. To put it very crudely: continuity is a 'good thing', and discontinuity is a 'bad thing'.

Is this assumption entirely valid? Consider one or two difficulties. The cry 'God mit uns' has been heard on countless battlefields, from the siege of Jericho to the Milvian bridge and Lepanto, from Vietnam to Belfast. If we wish to make a radical break from the view that God is, if not on the side of the big battalions, then at least on the side of the battalions of the elect (who, happily, always include us!), then it is not immediately obvious that we can do so in the name of continuity.

Or think of the Christ-Pantokrator of Byzantine art, of the Christ of Roualt's paintings, of the Christ on the tympanum at Chartres or Vézelay, of the wistful, nightgowned hermaphrodite of Victorian piety. How would it be possible for us so to conceive of God revealed in Christ as simultaneously to express our understanding by employing all these images? It is tempting to evade the issue by saying: Ah, but each of these images of Christ expresses some aspect of his inexhaustible mystery. There is an important element of truth in this, but it overlooks the fact that these images were the product and the expression of distinct, and often conflicting, conceptions and structures of man and society. To seek to employ them all simultaneously would be to seek to construct a social order which was at once Byzantine, compassionate, feudal and nineteenth-century bourgeois.

We may wish to emphasize the imperfection and provisionality of all visions of man, and of all forms of social and political organization. Fine. But we have to decide which vision to pursue, which social order to construct, here and now. We have to choose between models of man and of society. And, in the measure that we do so choose, we shall find that we are also choosing one 'model' of God rather than another, albeit that, in so doing, we are and must be acutely conscious of its inadequacy and provisionality.

Am I suggesting that our models of God are simply, as it were, ideological rhetoric? Certainly not, as I have already tried to make clear in earlier sections of this paper. But I am suggesting that we should recognize the unavoidable presence of an ideological component in our own understanding of God as in that of all previous generations of Christians. I shall come back to this problem later on. For the moment, I want to move on to a related issue more immediately connected with the assumption we are considering: the assumption, that is, that continuity is to be sought and fostered and discontinuity shunned and feared.

I have suggested that preoccupation with continuity arises out of a concern faithfully to hear the voice of a God whose definitive self-expression occurred in the past. But is it not possible that this preoccupation, thus accounted for, is also, in no small measure, the rationalization of a cultural nostalgia, a fear of change, disorder and chaos, a social and political conservatism? Thus it comes about that the God who once threatened the stability of the Roman Empire is appealed to in justification of the rejection of contemporary social and cultural change.

In such circumstances, a particular understanding of God, and of God's ways with man, is being employed (usually quite unwittingly) to shore up and conserve certain cultural values and existing political structures. (I say, 'usually quite unwittingly', although there are hilarious exceptions, such as the case of Mgr Nardi, of the Sacred Roman Rota, who pointed out, in 1869, that it was desirable to define the infallibility of the Pope because 'he who believes in a Pope believes in God, and he who believes in God would never conspire to overthrow a government'.)[4]

The point is, surely, that whenever, however high the motive or noble the cause, we seek to put God to *use*, then we have turned our back on him, ceased to listen to and worship him. Our understanding of 'God' is no longer the understanding of *God* at all. It is now pure ideology, an ideology all the more dangerous for being disguised as Christian faith. It is in respect of considerations such as these, I believe, that much Catholic and Anglican theological writing still needs injecting with a good dose of the paradoxes of Barthian evangelicalism!

The other side of the coin, of course, is that whereas an acceptance of confusion, of discontinuity, of the dissolution of certainties and the loss of bearings, may indeed be the expression of an irresponsible frivolity or a self-willed rejection of the historical enfleshment of God's Word and Spirit, it may also sometimes be a form of fidelity to that Word, of obedience to the promptings of that Spirit. When a correspondent once objected to Newman's fondness for speaking of the 'risk' and 'venture' of faith, Newman replied: 'Did not Abraham, my dear Sir, make a venture, when he went out, not knowing whither he went?'.[5]

But these last remarks have been improperly abstract and rhetorical. In the next section, I would like to try to pin them down a little, to spell them out with slightly greater precision.

Speaking in Situations

Bernard Lonergan has said that 'The key task ... in contemporary Catholic theology is to replace the shattered thought-

---

4 Cf. G. Thils, *L'Infaillibilité Pontificale: Sources – Conditions – Limites* (Gembloux, 1969), pp. 65–6.

5 C. S. Dessain, ed., *The Letters and Diaries of John Henry Newman, Vol. XII* (London, 1962), p. 168.

forms associated with eternal truths and logical ideals with new thoughtforms that accord with the dynamics of development and the concrete style of method'.[6] It once seemed that the ideal form of a theological statement was such that the statement would be timelessly, transculturally intelligible. In so far as this ideal was attained, doctrinal fidelity was necessarily expressed in the unswerving continuity, the maintained identity, of theological expression. Discontinuity would have been a departure from truth, a form of infidelity.

Thus Pope Paul VI, in the encyclical *Mysterium Fidei*, said that the concepts employed in dogmatic statements 'are not tied to any specific cultural system. . . . They are, therefore, within the reach of everyone at all times and in all places' (para. 24).

It is, however, increasingly evident that the ideal of timeless, transculturally available expressions of meaning is a chimera. We need to ask, of any statement: Who is making it, from where, and to whom? Speaker and listener alike inhabit particular worlds of experience, reference, affectivity, memory, presupposition and symbolic construction. And the 'meaning' of any statement, both the meaning which it has for the speaker and that which it has for the listener, is determined by the total concrete contexts from which and into which it is spoken.

(In passing, I might point out that thus to insist on the 'incarnate' nature of all human expressions of meaning and truth is not to open the floodgates to an unrestrained relativism according to which statements could only be 'true for me', or 'true for you', but never simply true. It may be the case that our expressions of meaning and truth are ineluctably situated, perspectival. It does not follow that, from within any particular situation, it is impossible to arrive at judgements that are, quite simply, true or false. If I say 'It is raining', this assertion is either true or false, but what you 'hear me saying' will be very different depending upon whether you are a farmer

6 B. J. F. Lonergan, 'Philosophy and Theology', *A Second Collection* (London, 1974), p. 202.

whose crops are withering from drought, or a lover who has asked, two seconds before, 'Do you still love me?')

I insisted earlier that, as Christians, we both can and must seek to speak, even today, of God. But then the question arises: How are we to do so? Except in a purely formal sense, there is no valid answer to that question which abstracts from our situation, and from that of the person, or group, whom we are addressing. Put it this way: the insistence that, as Christians, we can and must speak, today, of God, does not give us licence to say whatever we like, wherever and whenever we like, to whomever we like. Nor does it entitle us simply to repeat whatever our predecessors said, on the untroubled assumption that, in so doing, we shall, today, be speaking truly of God.

To speak is to speak to someone from somewhere. Thus, in order to discover the appropriate expression of Christian faith in any particular situation, there are two poles to be considered: the individual, or group, or institution, that seeks to communicate, and the individual, or group, or institution who are the intended recipients of the communication.

Perhaps these two poles can be indicated by saying that theological speech should aim at being, firstly, *responsible*, and, secondly, *intelligible*.

Responsible, inasmuch as the need to purify the ideological component in our understanding demands, amongst other things, that we seek critically to attend to, to appropriate, our own linguistic context – to grasp the presuppositions, implications, strengths, limitations, particular features of the world of action, organization, thought and symbolization that we inhabit. We need, so to say, continually to seek to make our situation 'transparent' to ourselves. We never wholly succeed: alienation, like other aspects of poverty, is always with us. But at least we can take seriously the fact that an essential precondition of responsible, faithful speech about God, witness to God, is a continual process of individual and corporate conversion, or *metanoia*. It is, perhaps, the continual need for *corporate*, institutional conversion that most needs to be stressed at this point, because it is this dimension of the problem which is most frequently overlooked in contemporary English theology. Following up a hint which I briefly threw out in the previous section, perhaps we can say: theological speech is irresponsible if it is 'satisfied' with whatever models of God, and of God's dealings with men, it employs or presupposes in any particular time or place. But *therefore* theological speech is irresponsible if its practitioners are 'satisfied' with the social order which such models symbolically refract. It is in considerations such as these, I believe, that the grounds of that political 'restlessness' (be its strategic expressions 'reformist' or 'revolutionary') which should characterize the prophetic dimension of Christianity are to be sought.[7]

Secondly, theological speech should aim at being intelligible. We need to know to whom we are speaking. And so, we seek to discover how to speak of God so that our interlocutor can hear, not necessarily what he expects or wants to hear, but what, given his previous experience, suffering, language, memory and hope, can be heard by him as the good news of the gospel.

(Just by way of a reminder that these problems are not the exclusive pain of *theological* speech: What does the rich man say of justice, and how does he say it, to the unemployed? What does the loved and cherished person say, and how does he say it, to the rejected and the bereaved? These are not merely rhetorical questions.)

What has all this got to do with the problem of continuity and discontinuity? The point can, I think, be quite simply made. It may well be the case, in any given situation, that that which we *can* say, responsibly and intelligibly, is not that which, were we to abstract from the two poles of concrete speech, we might have wished to say, or felt entitled or obliged to say. Consider two examples. Are there not many groups and individuals for whom, for a variety of historical reasons,

7 I have touched on this elsewhere in these essays: cf. the concluding paragraphs of 'Understanding the Stranger', and the section on 'The Church and Man's Freedom' in 'The Church and Christ's Freedom'.

almost any use by us of the term 'God', today, would ensure
that they did not, in fact, hear us speaking truly of *God?* Or
again: may it not sometimes be the case, for a variety of historical reasons, that the one place from which the gospel cannot
effectively be preached, today, is that institution charged with
the commission to preach the gospel in history?

In other words, may it not be the case, from time to time,
that the acceptance of discontinuities in both the language of
belief and in the 'location' of the place from which that language is spoken is a necessary condition of achieving, in practice, that fidelity to God's Word the pursuit of which accounts
for our concern for continuity?

Discontinuity, Faith and Theology

At the beginning of this paper, I said that I hoped to construct, in the final section, a tentatively sketched personal
response to the cluster of problems suggested by the title. This
response will take the form of a suggestion concerning the
'form of faith' appropriate in a cultural situation such as our
own, and concerning the relationship between faith and theology which should obtain in such a situation.

In the first place, I take it for granted that we are living in a
situation of profound and rapid linguistic, cultural and political change and upheaval. I take it for granted that we are in
the middle of, or possibly only in the very early stages of, one
of the most profound cultural, conceptual, structural revolutions that the world has ever known.

In such a situation, our experience is that of profound discontinuity, of a loss of bearings. We are living in the rubble of
a collapsing culture. The past is experienced, not as a rich
heritage to be fostered, but rather as a world profoundly
'other' than our own – whether the mood of this experience of
'otherness' be that of regret or rejection, puzzlement or unin-
terest. Where academics are concerned, in almost every discipline that is conscious of its historical dimension, the past is
experienced as 'unreadable', as 'opaque', except in so far as it

is handled *as* 'other', within the framework of one of a number of contemporary forms of thorough-going historicism. In other words, the past tends to be treated as *the* past rather than as *our* past. The confident, linear visions of development, evolution and progress that were characteristic of so much nineteenth-century thought have been replaced, in recent decades, by more fragmented, relativist structures of apprehension and analysis. In such a situation, 'continuity' is simply not, or at least is not at first sight, an intellectually or morally serious option, whether we like it or not.

Of course, ours is not the first social and cultural revolution in European history (even if I am right in thinking that the stakes are higher, the changes more profound, more fundamental, more global). It may therefore be helpful to glance back to an earlier revolution: that of the sixteenth and seventeenth centuries.

In a situation such as that which obtained in the sixteenth and seventeeth centuries, and that which obtains today, faith, for many, was and is no longer able to achieve linguistic and symbolic expression in the modes inherited from the past precisely because that past, as *experienced* in such a situation, has 'died', has become opaque and 'illegible'. Indeed, in such a situation, may it not be the case that directly and immediately to seek for an understanding of God, and thus for an appropriate mode of discourse concerning God, in continuity – in the language and form inherited from the past – would be to refuse to accept that a world had died, a culture corroded?

What is the alternative? May it not be that it is precisely *in* the ruins of that culture, *as* ruins, in the 'rubble' of discerned discontinuities, that faith might find an appropriate mode of apprehending God, and thus might find an appropriate form of discourse concerning God?

Is this redirection of faith's attention from a past rendered illegible to the wilderness of the present necessarily a rejection of the past? Or is it perhaps a hazardous attempt at fidelity? Unless a grain of wheat fall into the ground and die. . . .

In a situation in which continuity with the past is experienced as the dominant mode of the quest for meaning and truth, the model, the paradigm for success in that quest, for epistemological and linguistic achievement, is the 'wise man' or the 'expert', the bearer of tradition. Michel de Certeau, in a fascinating paper,[8] has pointed out that, for the mystical writers of the sixteenth and seventeenth centuries, the social types that dominated their discourse were, not the wise, but the mad, not the expert, but the children and the unlettered. It is, he says, as if for us today the 'heroes of knowledge' were the outcasts of society: the aged, the immigrant.[9]

In similar vein, Peter Berger has urged the necessity of rendering 'cognitive respect' to 'those who cannot claim the status of experts', on the grounds that, whereas 'expertise' is correlative to the technical handling, interpreting and assessing of data, 'there are no experts on the desirable goals of human life'.[10] Societies more confident than our own of their cognitive relationship with the past have not infrequently assumed that there are, even here, 'experts' to whom appeal can be made.

There is surely ample New Testament warrant for such a relocation of the paradigms of wisdom? At least it may be worth pointing out that 'dispossession', as a symbol of wisdom, is less likely to lead to the ideological and unfaithful 'putting of God to human use' than are those symbols which identify wisdom with the *possession* of truth.

One of the characteristic modes of discourse of the 'mystic', as distinct from the scholar, is the poem. Certain types of poetic utterance, unlike the work of scholarly interpretation are, in a sense, autonomous. As expressions of meaning and truth they 'stand on their own feet', whereas the work of scholarship necessarily appeals to, refers to, in a sense 'submits' to, sources, authorities, 'outside' itself. The scholar necessarily

8 M. de Certeau, 'L'Enonciation Mystique', *Recherches de Science Religieuse*, lxiv, 2 (1976), pp. 183–215.
9 de Certeau, art. cit., p. 192.
10 P. L. Berger, *Pyramids of Sacrifice: Political Ethics and Social Change* (London, 1976), p. 76.

stands 'within a tradition' in a sense that the poet does not. I would emphasize: 'in a sense'. All language, poetic or scholarly, as a social phenomenon, is ineluctably historical. If the poet stood outside all traditions he would be wholly unintelligible: his products would not be *language* at all. Nevertheless, the strategic distinction at which I am hinting is not without importance. The scholar, in order to be a scholar, necessarily 'has his eyes on the past', whereas the poet's gaze, however much he seeks to work within a tradition, is more immediately and sharply focussed on the present.

Perhaps the health, the flourishing, of faith's understanding, of Christian discourse concerning God, cries out with particular urgency in a time such as ours for poetic and prophetic statement. Perhaps poetic discourse, articulating the felt experience of Christians in a situation of cultural upheaval, would be a surer guarantee of the faithfulness of our Christian speech than scholarship alone could be.

Am I being uncharacteristically anti-intellectual? I think not. I am arguing for the priority of living faith in respect of theology, of poetic discourse in respect of scholarly interpretation. I am, therefore, doing little more than to endorse Newman's view of the relationship between 'religion' and 'theology'.[11] But there is something else that needs to be said. Poetry is not only, compared to scholarship, 'autonomous'; it is also, as 'autonomous', as the immediate articulation of present experience, anhistorical. Is not one of the most striking features of much contemporary interest in 'religious experience', from transcendental meditation to the charismatic movement, from Bultmann to popular Buddhism, its anhistoricality? This is the 'discourse of discontinuity'. And if it is entirely appropriate as the mood or form of faith's immediate, spontaneous quest for linguistic and conceptual expression, it is insufficient as the *only* mood or form of Christian discourse. However 'opaque' and 'illegible' the past, a faith that locates its source and strength in history, and in particular historical

11 For some comments on this, cf. below, 'Life, Language and Organisation'.

persons and events, can never surrender the attempt, however arduous its undertaking, to discover the continuities, to 'read' the past, to sustain the tradition. This attempt to discover the continuities, which is a permanent responsibility for Christian theology, will, however, be less neurotically, less *anxiously* pursued in the measure that truth, all truth, and *a fortiori* the truth of God, is sought as gift, and not clung to as personal or group possession. The model of the relationship between faith and theology which I am recommending is, I suggest, not anti-intellectual but anti-rationalist.

Therefore, whereas it is sometimes argued that unless theologians and scholars can discern, establish and secure the continuities, Christian belief becomes, in our day, impossible, I wish to reverse the emphasis and to suggest something like the following pattern of relationships between faith and theology. Faith can afford to risk seeking its mode of apprehension, and thus its mode of discourse, in the 'rubble' of cultural discontinuity in the measure that it lives in reciprocally interactive tension with a theology that seeks *its* mode of apprehension and discourse in the (otherwise 'opaque') continuities of history, and of social and institutional reality. Faith, thus conceived, is, without theology, anhistorical and anarchically autonomous, unreferred, unrooted. Theology, without faith, is either (in a situation such as ours) impossible, or else it is the 'chatter of fools' concerning a God whose presence has not been and cannot be discerned.

3. CAN A THEOLOGIAN KEEP THE FAITH?

Very few disciplines, today, are free from an element of methodological uncertainty, but there seem to be few areas in which questions of method are currently as confused as they are in theology. Many disciplines seem at least to be moderately clear about the nature and scope of their subject-matter. But if one asks: 'What is the subject-matter of theology?', it is not at all clear what the answer ought to be. The aim of the present paper, therefore, is necessarily a very restricted one: to break up the ground a little, raising many problems and dealing adequately with none, in order to suggest the context in which one might reflect on the sort of thing which would count as evidence for the claims of Christian belief, and on the way in which that evidence might show itself.[1]

According to John Macquarrie: 'Theological language arises out of religious language as a whole, and it does so when religious faith becomes reflective and tries to give an account of itself in verbal statements.'[2] While I am not entirely happy about the implied restriction of theological statements to second-order statements, I think that that description is helpful in that it implies a distinction between the status of faith-claims and the status of second-order theological assertions. In other words, the assertion 'I believe in God' is not necessar-

1 This paper, originally a contribution to an interdisciplinary seminar, held at St Edmund's House, Cambridge, on problems of 'proof and evidence', was first published as 'Can a Methodologist Keep the Faith?', *Irish Theological Quarterly*, xxxviii (1971), pp. 91–102.
2 J. Macquarrie, *God-Talk* (London, 1967), p. 19.

ily shown to be incoherent by the fact that attempts to explain what is meant by 'I believe in God' are often extremely confused. I am not nearly as puzzled by people who say 'I believe in God' as I am by people who think that they can give a straightforward and satisfactory account of what they mean when they say that they believe in God.

Bernard Lonergan, in a characteristically lapidary phrase, has said that 'method is simply reason's explicit consciousness of the norms of its own procedures'.[3] Taking our cue from Lonergan, then, we might say that the believing mind only becomes theological (in Macquarrie's sense) in so far as it becomes explicitly conscious of the norms of its own procedures. The question 'Can a theologian keep the faith?' seems to imply that if a believer becomes reflectively aware of what he is 'doing', in believing, then he may feel obliged to stop doing it. However, there seem to be at least four options open to the believer who becomes, as it were, methodologically alert.

Firstly, he may decide that the criticisms brought to bear upon the claims of Christian belief by the historian, the philosopher, the psychologist, and so on, are so devastating that he has no alternative but to renounce those claims, in other words: to declare himself a non-believer. This is clearly a position in which an increasing number of people find themselves. It does not usually find expression in full-blown theoretical atheism, but in that practical atheism which is a form of agnosticism. We should, perhaps, ask ourselves whether it is obviously the case that Christian belief systematically excludes all forms of agnosticism.

Secondly, the believer may decide that religious belief is *sui generis* to such an extent that only the believer is competent to evaluate criticisms based on non-religious criteria or formulated within a non-religious perspective. He can therefore afford to let the waves of criticism batter on the rock of his

3 B. J. F. Lonergan, 'Theology and Understanding', *Collection* (London, 1967), p. 138.

unshakeable certainty. He knows what he believes, and that is an end to it.

Thirdly, he may decide that, while the criticisms of the historian, the philosopher and the psychologist are significant, and cannot be ignored, nevertheless they are neither destructive nor do they necessitate withdrawal into the immune citadel of the fideist. So far as the historian is concerned, he may decide that there is still available to him an apologetic which is sufficient for his purposes. So far as the philosopher is concerned, he may want to say, with Van Buren: 'It may be too strong to say (of modern philosophers) that they have been working with the religious language learned in Sunday school, but the theologian cannot help feeling that the most serious problems have not been dealt with when the logical difficulty of saying "There is a God", or "God exists" is pointed out.'[4]

There may, however, be a fourth option open, a fourth type of reaction to the pressures of methodological awareness. A person who wished to take this option might sympathize with the third group inasmuch as he recognized that the critics of Christian belief do not always seem to be fully aware of their own presuppositions or of the complexity of the notion of faith. He might sympathize with the second group inasmuch as there does seem to be a certain qualified immunity which faith claims, even if it is not the radical immunity of the fideist. He might sympathize with the first group inasmuch as it is difficult to know whether one is a believer or an unbeliever until one knows which of the many current conceptions of religious belief or unbelief one is being invited to espouse. As Leslie Dewart has said: 'in the Christian tradition, *which* God we believe in is of the utmost importance'.[5] The root problem seems to be the nature of religious certainty. That Christians, throughout history, have claimed in some way to be certain about something, seems to be true. But what it is that they are certain about, and in what way they might propose to justify

4 P. Van Buren, *The Secular Meaning of the Gospel* (London, 1968), p. 109.
5 L. Dewart, *The Future of Belief* (London, 1967), p. 68.

that certainty – about these things there is very little agreement.

It may help to clear the ground a little if we look briefly at two of the types of criticism to which 'belief in God' is currently subjected. The examples I have chosen are those of the philosopher and the historian, as represented by Paul Van Buren and Van Harvey.

Van Buren is not sceptical about the possibility of belief, but about the possibility of articulating that belief in 'transcendence-talk'. According to him, 'modern man' only uses empirical and 'this-worldly' language. Therefore, if we are to enable him to sustain and articulate his belief, we must attempt to reduce theological language to its historical and ethical dimensions.[6] Van Buren's concern is not apologetic but pastoral. That is to say: he is not directly concerned with attempting to 'prove' anything to the man outside the Church. 'Our question', he says, 'has to do with the "modern man" who is inside the church, more or less, and who is wondering what he is doing there.'[7]

'The crux of Van Buren's whole argument can be expressed in two consecutive propositions: first, it is impossible to talk empirically about God; secondly, and the man of today must always talk empirically.'[8] I shall assume that the first proposition is broadly acceptable in the sense that God is not a fact in the world. The second proposition, however, is questionable, from two points of view. In the first place, to say that the language of 'modern man' is primarily concerned with the factual and the verifiable, which seems to be true of many 'modern men', is not the same as to say that the only universe of discourse which is available to 'modern man' is that of straightforward empirical assertion.

The second difficulty I have about the way in which Van Buren describes contemporary empiricism or 'secularity' is more difficult to get into focus. God is not a fact in the world.

6 Cf. Van Buren, op. cit., p. 198.
7 Ibid., p. 24.
8 R. L. Richard, *Secularization Theology* (London, 1967), p. 109.

But Van Buren seems to assume that statements about God are statements, as it were, about *another* order of facts existing 'beyond' or 'outside' this world. That many Christians do talk about God in this way I do not deny, nor is the analysis of such language my immediate concern. But I would want to question the apparent assumption that the horizons of empirical discourse, and therefore of the world, are necessarily closed and static. That our experience is limited, is true. That the questions, hopes and possibilities to which our experience gives rise, are similarly limited, I would wish to deny.

However, even if it is the case that philosophical criticisms raised against the possibility of theological discourse are not so totally devastating as they are sometimes claimed to be, it does not seem that this would entitle the believer to claim immunity from the philosopher's questions. To talk about God has never been easy; today it is, if not impossible, at least exceedingly difficult. But does this mean, bringing back a distinction which was made at the beginning of this paper, that *belief* is exceedingly difficult? Or, to put it another way, does it mean that the difficulty of believing is exactly the *same* difficulty as that involved in articulating or discursively justifying that belief?

Part of the reason why, for Van Buren, as for most other Christians, the answer to that question is 'No', is that 'Faith is', as he says, 'dependent upon the event of Jesus Christ, his appearance in history, his words and death'.[9] Methodologically, I should wish to urge the view that specifically Christian faith-claims are not firstly claims about the existence or non-existence of something or someone called God, which are then providentially strengthened by certain events in Palestine. It is the other way round. Christian faith, like the faith of the Old Testament, is generated from the experience of salvation, and is structured as a response to, and an interpretation of the history within which that experience of salvation takes place. Central to this response and interpretation are certain events

9 Van Buren, op. cit., p. 19.

which took place in Palestine. The occurrence of these events does not necessarily entail that the response which is made to them by the Christian believer, or the interpretation which he gives to them, are justified. But if these events did not take place, then it is not clear to what he is responding or what he is interpreting. In other words, in so far as an element of historical factuality is inescapably bound up with the claims of Christian belief, the believer has to meet the questions and the criticisms of the historian.

One scholar who has met these questions with both honesty and clarity is Van Harvey. In order to feel the force of the problem with which he grapples in an excellent book, it is not necessary to adopt his own conclusion, which is that 'if we understand properly what is meant by faith, then this faith has no clear relation to any particular set of historical beliefs at all.'[10] He leans heavily on Troeltsch, who perceived, he says, that 'the historical method is but the expression of a new morality of critical judgement ... which seems incompatible with the ethic of belief that has dominated Christendom for centuries'.[11] What this criticism amounts to is the charge that 'orthodox belief corrodes the delicate machinery of sound historical judgement'.[12] Why? Because, even in the limit case, the historian's conclusions are statements of probability, or what Harvey calls 'soft assents'. How, then, is it possible for the Christian to ground the 'hard assent', the life and death commitment of faith, upon the evidence presented to him by the historian? If the historian can only say, for example, that it is reasonably certain that a man called Jesus lived in Palestine, and that he was killed; that there are very few statements of which we can say with any great degree of probability that they were made by Jesus; that there is strong, but ambiguous evidence that his friends reacted strangely after his death, and appear to have been convinced that, although he had died, he

10 V. A. Harvey, *The Historian and the Believer* (London, 1967), p. 280.
11 Harvey, op. cit., p. 38.
12 Ibid., p. 119.

lived still – how can the Christian acquire that certainty concerning these facts, and their significance, which would be sufficient to make him leave parents, friends and possessions, and even to surrender his life?

Now, even if we grant that many historians investigating the historical component of the ground of Christian belief are negatively affected by their own presuppositions, this does not cause the problem to evaporate. What are we to make of statements such as: 'We need not be too frightened by the historian's conclusions, because we trust the Church'? In so far as such statements imply the possession by Christians of grounds for historical judgements which are not available to historians they are, I believe, to be rejected. To say this, however, is not to resolve the extremely difficult problem of establishing the criteria according to which evidence is admitted and evaluated in the interpretation of doctrinal history.

It was suggested earlier that the problems posed by the philosopher were directly problems for theology and only indirectly problems for faith. It seems clear, however, that the problems posed by the historian strike at the very possibility of Christian belief. In attempting, very briefly, to indicate why, in spite of taking seriously the historian's questions, I do not feel impelled to reach conclusions similar to Harvey's concerning the relationship of faith to historical beliefs, it may be helpful to invoke Cardinal Newman as counsel for the defence. He did, after all, in both the *University Sermons* and the *Grammar of Assent,* try to grapple with this issue. And the fact that critical historiography has developed new tools and new sensitivities in the last hundred years does not necessarily mean that he has nothing helpful to contribute.

In the *University Sermons,* Newman's chief antagonist is the rationalist who would maintain that, if faith is to be other than mere credulity and superstition, then the evidence on which it rests must be securely demonstrated and arguments based on the evidence must be explicitly stated and rigorously analysed. In other words, before I can reasonably believe, I must not only have good reasons for believing, but I must have them in such a way that I can personally discursively demonstrate the rationality of my belief.

It is important to remember that, in building up his critique of the rationalist position, Newman is concerned to justify, not simply religious belief, but belief in general. For Newman, believing my friends, believing the newspapers, and believing God, are – structurally – the same kind of disposition or activity. This is why he said, as early as 1829, that 'When faith is said to be a religious principle, it is ... the things believed, not the act of believing them, which is peculiar to religion'.[13] And the same conviction is one of the dominant features of the architecture of the *Grammar of Assent,* forty years later.[14]

Newman's dissatisfaction with the rationalist's demand for prior demonstration of the grounds of belief is doubly motivated. In the first place, if the rationalist's position were correct, only a scholar could be a non-credulous believer: 'If children, if the poor, if the busy, can have true faith, yet cannot weigh evidences, evidence is not the simple foundation on which Faith is built.'[15]

In the second place, and this is fundamental: 'Faith is a principle of action, and action does not leave time for minute and finished investigations.'[16] As a result, faith always requires courage; it involves taking a risk; it is – and this is a favourite word of his – a 'venture'. He does not regard the risk-laden, venturesome nature of faith as a weakness, but as a strength. Growing in belief is, in some sense, the acquisition of a skill – hence the famous analogy of the mountain-climber in the thirteenth of the *University Sermons.*[17]

13 J. H. Newman, *Parochial and Plain Sermons, Vol. I* (London, 1868), p. 191.
14 In·my introduction to the University of Notre Dame Press's recent (1979) edition of the *Grammar of Assent,* I have sketched the background and highlighted the principal features of Newman's treatment of religious 'certitude'.
15 J. H. Newman, *Fifteen Sermons Preached Before the University of Oxford* (London, 1871), p. 231.
16 Newman, *University Sermons,* p. 188.
17 Cf. ibid., p. 257.

If one is prepared to go this far with Newman, the next question would seem to be: is it not proper for faith to seek safeguards? The answer to that question depends upon the kind of safeguards for which one seeks. The rationalist will insist that faith is safeguarded and improved by rigorous demonstration both of its grounds (through historical enquiry) and of the logic of its procedures (through philosophical enquiry). Newman does not deny that such analysis has a useful function to perform, but he sees this function as being essentially derivative; he twice likens it to the function of literary criticism in respect of poetry.[18] Such an analysis would be a theological activity, in the sense in which theology was described at the beginning of this paper. Now, however useful and even indispensable theology may be, it is not, for Newman, the *safeguard* of faith. Again and again he insists that the safeguard of faith is loving obedience, in other words, practice: a style of life.

If theology is, amongst other things, belief giving an account of itself in verbal statements, and if belief has the qualities of risk, trust and venture which, following Newman, have just been described, it becomes important to ask: is belief, Christian belief, itself a cognitive activity?

The short answer to that question is: Yes. However, in view of the complexity of the question, and of the active and confused debate which currently surrounds it, it is not possible here to do more than crudely and schematically suggest a way in which that affirmative answer might be elaborated.

In saying that Christian belief *is* a cognitive activity, I am denying that it is simply an attitude of blind, unaccountable, emotional trust.

In saying that Christian belief is a cognitive activity, I am not saying that the Christian believer claims access, at least in any very obvious sense, to data which are not also available to the nonbeliever. After all, the historical components in the content of Christian belief, their scriptural or credal interpre-

---

18 Cf. ibid., pp. 184, 321–2.

tation, the liturgical embodiment of that interpretation – all these things are surely available as a source of reflection for anybody.

What about that approach to the problem which one associates with John Hick, to the effect that Christian belief is cognitive, not in respect of this or that item of information or field of data, but as a total interpretation of the world and its history?[19] On this view of things, Christian faith is an attitude towards the world which shows itself as cognitive inasmuch as it finds expression in metaphysical assertions which, it is claimed, will be authenticated or verified at the coming of God's kingdom.

There is much that is attractive in this kind of approach, but I am puzzled by Van Buren when, adopting a similar approach, he says: 'The choice of a non-cognitive, "blik" conception of faith, rather than of a cognitive conception, will be fundamental to our study.'[20] This is puzzling both because Van Buren does, surely correctly, make statements about Jesus and his death and resurrection which seem to embody truth-claims, and because he himself, in another passage, says: 'A call to faith that depreciates thinking and logical reflection is a call to a quite different sort of "blik" from the one of which we have been speaking. It would be a perspective without historical foundation, a feeling or orientation which could give no logical account of itself.'[21]

Perhaps what he has in mind when he calls faith 'non-cognitive' is the fact that, as he says, 'the issue between those whose perspective on life and history is defined by the history of Jesus and those whose perspective is defined by another reference is notoriously one that cannot be settled by argument'.[22] In other words, someone may bring arguments against a position which I hold and yet, for all their clarity and cogency, they may not dispose me to abandon my position.

19 Cf. J. Hick, *Faith and Knowledge* ([2] London, 1967).
20 Van Buren, op. cit., p. 102.
21 Ibid., p. 175.
22 Ibid., pp. 144–5.

Why? Because my position and that from within which the criticism arose may be seen, not infrequently, to be grounded in two very different perspectives or frames of reference. This seems to be the kind of situation in which the believer may claim that qualified immunity (though the word is probably too strong) to which I referred earlier.

In what does this element of 'immunity' consist? Perhaps a clue may be found in the suggestion which, following Newman, I made a little earlier: namely, that there are similarities between growth in faith and the acquisition of a skill. This suggestion will, perhaps, only be surprising to those whose preoccupation with epistemological problems concerning the nature and object of 'acts' of faith has tended to make them underestimate the extent to which, in large areas of Christian theological tradition, the 'act' of faith is seen, as it were, as the precipitate of the skill, 'virtue' or *'habitus'* of faith. Awareness of the importance of cognitional attitudes and acquired habits is not limited to the students of Christian belief and understanding. There are similarities between the significance of the analogy of the mountain-climber for Newman, and that of the piano-player for Polanyi.[23]

The relevance of this aspect of belief for the problem of the 'immunity' of that belief is, I suggest, that the attitudes and approaches to life of any particular group of people are notoriously difficult to share with other people whose own experience and history has been significantly different. It may well be, therefore, that the believer is entitled to treat with reserve such criticisms, whether philosophical or historical, as spring from an experience and a history different from his own. It would, of course, be seriously to misunderstand this suggestion if it were taken as an endorsement of that obscurantism which has too often been a feature of Christian belief and theology.

Appeals to individual, private experience are unhelpful because they simply cannot be discussed. Appeals to shared

23 M. Polanyi, *The Tacit Dimension* (London, 1967), pp. 9–19.

experience, to the way in which a particular group of people have come to understand and evaluate their life and history, have a different status. Such appeals are to an experience which is public at least in so far as it has become articulate in the language of the group. While it is true that a 'private language' is a contradiction in terms, it also seems to be true that there is, in fact, no such thing as a wholly public language, equally and immediately available to all men, wherever they may be. (By 'language' I mean not simply verbal signs, but the whole complex of words, music, art, architecture, gesture and silence by means of which a group of people experience and achieve their common mediation of meaning and purpose as a human community.) In other words, a completely shared experience, common to all men, expressing itself in a common language and a common set of judgements and consequent commitments, is not the presupposition of valid attempts at discourse, but is rather the goal of human and Christian hope.[24]

When I refer to Christian belief as a 'skill', therefore, I mean that it is a way of seeing things, an intellectual and practical stance in respect of the world and its history, and in particular in respect of certain critical events or moments in that history, which can – in the ordinary way – only be acquired and sustained in the context of a common life and common activity. The weakness of much apologetic argument is that it pretends that this climate of common experience, this fragile understanding and the judgements which flow from it, can be persuasively demonstrated to somebody who does not share the life which is its presupposition.

Now, because that interpretation of history which is the cognitive component in Christian belief extends, in some sense, to an interpretation of all things and of the future, it can only find expression in symbolic forms. And this is what the liturgy does. The celebration of the liturgy is the primary context within which the articulation of Christian belief is

24 Cf. Bernard Lonergan's discussion of community as 'an achievement of common meaning', in '*Existenz* and *Aggiornamento*', *Collection*, p. 245.

attempted, and not the least important of the tasks of theology, preaching and prayer is reflection on the significance of these symbolic forms.[25]

Although the problem of the nature of that certainty which faith claims underlies many of the problems which have been too briefly touched upon in this paper, it has not yet been raised explicitly. In order to do so, two questions may be asked: Is theology threatened today? and, Is faith threatened today?

Is theology threatened today? Yes, and from at least two points of view. In the first place, as was suggested earlier, the sheer complexity and difficulty of the historical and philosophical issues involved necessarily makes theology an exceedingly fragile and provisional business.

In the second place, theology, as a form of common language, is threatened to the extent that *all* common language is currently threatened and rendered problematic.

Is faith threatened today? At the beginning of the paper, it was claimed that the fact that theology becomes more difficult does not necessarily mean that faith becomes impossible. However, if theology became *impossible*, faith would also become impossible, and increasing difficulty in theology does make it increasingly difficult to believe. To say that Christian belief is a rational activity is at least to point to the fact that it is inexorably driven to seek rational articulation in the language of theology. The extreme difficulty of this articulation may drive the Christian back into the silence of belief, but so long as he insists on the *possibility* of theology, he is insisting that, in some sense, belief is a rational activity.

Although, throughout this paper, I have been implying a rather sharp distinction between faith and theology, it would clearly be a mistake to forget that the relationship and degree of interaction between them is a great deal tighter than some defenders of 'simple faith' would have us believe. To put it very simply: the harder it is to talk together, the harder it is to

25 Cf. N. L. A. Lash, *His Presence in the World* (London, 1968), Ch.I.

live and work and hope together, and therefore the harder it is to believe.

A thorough examination of the issues with which this paper is concerned would have to tackle the question: What is the place of the concepts of 'grace' and the 'action of the Spirit' in a discussion of the evidence for the claims of Christian belief? Is it not the case that many Christians would attribute their certainty of belief to the action of God's Spirit within them, to the experience of grace? The importance of such questions is that they remind us that the manner in which Christian beliefs – *as* religious beliefs, as expressions of trust in the mystery of the living God – are *held*, is such as to suggest a very close relationship, in practice, between 'believing' and 'praying', between 'faith' and 'prayerfulness'. The difficulty of such questions consists in the fact that, in order to discuss them adequately, it would be necessary to raise again all the problems with which this paper has been concerned, and to do so in a different conceptual and linguistic framework. All that I have offered in this paper is a sketch of the problem of 'evidence' from the standpoint of the phenomenology of belief, not from the standpoint of a theological account of faith's radical dependence on the presence and action of God.

The certainty which is proper to faith has more in common with the certainty that characterizes profound human relationships than it does with the certainty with which we hold particular propositions that we have come to accept as true (which is not to deny that 'personal' certitudes entail propositional claims; that 'real' assents entail 'notional' assents). As such, it is a certainty which enables and encourages risk and insecurity, and not a certainty which obliterates them. To say that we are 'certain of God' is to say that we know him as 'he who saves'. Our faith in God, our certainty concerning God, is mediated across the texture of the common life of a community dedicated to hearing his saving Word, and keeping it in faithful service. We have come back, once again, to Newman's insistence that faith is safeguarded only by loving obedience. It is only possible to sustain belief in the possibility of our future in God in the measure that we are concerned about, and engaged in the construction of that future. Blondel expressed it beautifully: '"To keep" the word of God means in the first place to do it, to put it into practice; and the deposit of Tradition ... cannot be transmitted in its entirety, indeed, cannot be used and developed, unless it is confided to the practical obedience of love.'[26]

Can a theologian keep the faith? If our notion of faith is that of unassailable security through the affirmation of propositions for which immunity is claimed from philosophical and historical criticism, then I believe that the answer is: No. In many respects, the withdrawal of the fideist into his world of private certainties is a greater betrayal of Christian faith than the open-ended insecurity of the agnostic.

If, however, it is permissible to speak of faith in the way in which I have attempted to do, then I believe that the answer is: Yes. But we can only provisionally demonstrate that this is the right answer by taking the risks entailed in the exploration and construction of our human future; risks which we are impelled to take inasmuch as, through our celebration of the liturgy, we find that the death and resurrection of Christ permanently and inescapably confront us with questions and provoke us to activity.

And we cannot *prove* that 'Yes' is the right answer until we arrive at that total transformation of the human condition which will make faith unnecessary and proof irrelevant. The theologian, or anybody else for that matter, can only hope to keep faith until the kingdom comes.

26 M. Blondel, 'History and Dogma', *The Letter on Apologetics and History and Dogma*, presented and translated by A. Dru and I. Trethowan (London, 1964), p. 274.

4. UNDERSTANDING THE STRANGER[1]

'Hermeneutics and the study of history are basic to all human science. Meaning enters into the very fabric of human living but varies from place to place and from one age to another.'[2] At the present time, Lonergan points out, a number of factors have combined to heighten enormously the problem of interpretation. Amongst the factors that he mentions are an increasing awareness, on the one hand, of the fact that many different cultures, or contexts of meaning, co-exist at the present time and, on the other hand, of the great differences that separate present from past cultures.[3]

However, the complexity of the task of interpretation is not simply due to our recognition of an irreducible pluralism in the *interpretandum*. It is also due to the fact that the interpreters themselves, as inhabitants of different disciplinary, linguistic and epistemological contexts and traditions, work with a variety of distinct notions of interpretation. I say 'notions' rather than 'theories' because not all those directly engaged in interpretative activities – as biblical exegetes, historians, anthropologists or sociologists – reflexively appropriate the hermeneutical notions with which they operate, in order to give to those notions formal theoretical expression.

Pannenberg has argued, persuasively, that what is at issue, as between Lonergan and the Diltheyan tradition of hermeneutics, are the contrasting theories of meaning which

1 First published in the *Irish Theological Quarterly*, xli (1974), pp. 91–103.
2 B. J. F. Lonergan, *Method in Theology* (London, 1972), p. 81.
3 Cf. ibid., p. 154.

underlie different conceptions of the task of interpretation.[4] In other words, not only does meaning vary 'from place to place and from one age to another', but the meaning of meaning is variously, and not uniformly, conceived in our own age (and even in our own place).

For this reason, amongst others, the descriptive accuracy of a theory of interpretation is restricted by the particular cultural, linguistic and epistemological context from which it emerges. The more generalized the theory, the more it will tend to have normative, rather than descriptive status, and the more questionable will be the authority of its prescriptions. What, then, are the choices open to us? We could, of course, choose simply to ignore the radical pluralism of contemporary contexts of meaning. Cambridge, Tübingen, Paris or Buenos Aires could go about their business as if Buenos Aires, Paris, Tübingen or Cambridge (or any one of them) simply did not exist. Or, to cut the cake another way, exegetes, philosophers of natural science, anthropologists and sociologists of knowledge could insist that what the others were doing was of no interest or significance to themselves.

There is, I believe, another route open to us. Instead of setting our sights on the generation of ever more satisfying hermeneutical theory from within the safety of our particular cultural or disciplinary frontiers, we can ask whether there is to be discerned, in the hermeneutical praxis of very different disciplines, methods and epistemologies, a measure of potential agreement concerning those aspects of the problem of interpretation which should most urgently command our attention today. What we are looking for, then, is some evidence of convergence in the concerns which dictate hermeneutical practice.

My initial aim, in this paper, is to suggest that some such convergence does exist. In recent years, widely differing forms of hermeneutical practice have independently converged on

4 Cf. W. Pannenberg, 'History and Meaning in Bernard Lonergan's Approach to Theological Method', *Looking at Lonergan's Method*, ed. P. Corcoran (Dublin, 1975), pp. 88–100.

the problem of the apparent incommensurability of statements, beliefs and theories, generated in significantly different
cultural contexts. It is not simply the *plurality* of contexts of
meaning of which we have become acutely conscious. More
specifically, it is the *discontinuity* between these contexts which
has moved to the centre of our hermeneutical concern. In
philosophy, in the history of science, in the social sciences, in
historiography, in theology, we are no longer confident that
we can understand the stranger.

(Even his staunchest disciples would not claim that the
amazing influence of Thomas Kuhn's *Structure of Scientific
Revolutions* can be attributed to its theoretical precision. But,
for that very reason, the widespread attraction of Kuhn's
thesis, as a model articulating the felt hermeneutical concerns
of a variety of different disciplines, neatly underscores the
point that I am making.[5])

Meaning in History

My suggestion, then, is that the fact or possibility of radical
discontinuity between different contexts of meaning has
become a primary focus of concern for a wide range of distinct
hermeneutical practices.[6] In order to give this suggestion less
abstract expression, I would now like to offer a brief historical
sketch of the manner in which, during the past hundred years,
this situation has come about.

Let us imagine, for a moment, that differences in cultural
and social context do *not* significantly determine man's consciousness and cognitive procedures,[7] and that all men, of all

5 Cf. T. S. Kuhn, *The Structure of Scientific Revolutions* (Chicago, 1962). For
an illustration of this use of Kuhn, see Philip Pettit, 'French Philosophy', *The Cambridge Review* (June, 1973), pp. 178–80; a lucid statement of
the incommensurability of English and French philosophical methods
and concerns.

6 Where problems of doctrinal change and continuity are concerned, I
have tried to pursue this discussion in N. L. A. Lash, *Change in Focus*
(London, 1973).

7 According to Peter Berger, the 'root proposition' of the sociology of

times, in all places, think more or less the same way. There is then in principle no disquieting 'gap' to be bridged by the would-be interpreter. We can approach the task of understanding any text, from any period, with untroubled confidence. Its author is assumed to perceive, and to think, and to argue, more or less as we do. The notion of a plurality of contexts of meaning, and of forms of cognitive procedure, has not occurred to us. If we then find that the author's patterns of argument, and the conclusions at which he arrives, are seemingly unintelligible or incorrect, we assume not that we have failed to understand him, but that his procedures are faulty. We judge his conclusions to be meaningless or false, and his argumentation defective in logic or in rationality. (Indeed, if the person whom we seek to understand is, not a dead author, but a living contemporary, we judge him to be certainly unorthodox, probably confused and possibly insane.)

During the nineteenth century, however, deepening historical consciousness increasingly forced the interpreter to pay serious attention to the historical and social context of the reported beliefs or statements which he sought to understand. It became increasingly clear that not all men, of all times and all places, had thought like nineteenth-century European intellectuals. For the first time, inhabitants of other cultural contexts were experienced, hermeneutically, as 'strangers'. But how were the differences to be accounted for?

Theoretically, it would have been possible to decide that the stranger was simply irrational. Not the least awkward feature of this conclusion would have been that it threatened the widespread belief in the fundamental homogeneity of 'human nature'. The infant social sciences, therefore, appealed to the genetic models which characterized nineteenth-century historical consciousness, and came up with a somewhat less drastic answer. 'The differences between western societies and those taken to be primitive could be ascribed simply to the low stage

---

knowledge, a proposition 'derived from Marx', is that 'man's consciousness is determined by his social being', P. L. Berger and T. Luckmann, *The Social Construction of Reality* (London, Penguin Books, 1971), p. 17.

of development at which the latter had succeeded in arriving: savages were potentially capable of civilization, and of the correct rationality characteristic of this achievement, but at their actual point of evolution their thoughts were, as Morgan, for example, concluded, feeble in degree and limited in range, and their intelligence was infantile.'[8]

In the theology of the period, an extensive reliance on organic imagery, according to which contemporary Christianity was seen as the 'fruit' or 'flower' of the 'seed' or 'germ' once planted in Palestine, encouraged the assumption that nineteenth-century Christianity was more advanced than, and hence in some respects superior to, the early Church. It did not occur to liberal theologians that there was any difficulty, in principle, in understanding the early Church. It *was* understood, and was understood – significantly – to have been the 'primitive' Church (even if the more unwelcome implications of this assessment were avoided by investing its primitivity with a romantic and historically unconvincing aura of primeval innocence and virtue).

Common to both theology and the other sciences was the 'assumption of an absolute superiority inherent in European modes of thought'.[9] In the social sciences, one of the first to break away from this assumption was Lévy-Bruhl, whose 'main theoretical merit was ... that he took seriously the possibility that "the fundamental identity of human nature", a premise on which he quite explicitly based his investigations, might nevertheless be "compatible with the existence of mentalities that were sharply different one from another" '.[10] 'The true burden of Lévy-Bruhl's arguments ... was therefore that ... other civilizations presented us with *alternative* categories and modes of thought.'[11]

---

8 R. Needham, *Belief, Language and Experience* (Oxford, 1972), p. 160. The reference is to Lewis H. Morgan's introduction to L. Fison and A. W. Howitt, *Kamilaroi and Kurnai* (Melbourne, 1880).
9 Needham, op. cit., p. 182.
10 Ibid., p. 167, quoting L. Lévy-Bruhl, *La Mentalité Primitive* (Oxford, 1931), p. 8.
11 Needham, op. cit., p. 183.

Thus, the increasing recognition of a pluralism of contexts of meaning, a recognition which characterized the emergence of the social sciences, gave rise to various forms of epistemological relativism. Today, the positivism of structuralist modes of analysis is one such form; the post-Wittgensteinian tradition represented, for example, by Peter Winch's *Idea of a Social Science*,[12] is another.

One of the more extreme recent expressions of a profound awareness of the intractability of the problem of understanding the stranger is Rodney Needham's *Belief, Language and Experience*. 'I am not saying', says Needham, 'that human life is senseless, but that we cannot make sense of it. . . . Once outside a given form of life, man is lost in a "wildernesse of formes".'[13]

In the same vein, Mary Hesse has remarked, in a lecture to the British Academy, that, 'The thought forms of alien cultures may be so foreign to our own that it might make sense to say that I understand my dog, or even my chrysanthemums, better than I understand those people'.[14]

I have suggested that, in all the human sciences, including theology, the characteristic response to the initial recognition of hermeneutical problems was ethnocentric in form: that is to say, the categories and modes of thought of the interpreter were, in practice, regarded as normative. In the social sciences, the present century has seen ethnocentric assumptions give way, first to various forms of relativism and, eventually, to the admission of the possibility that hermeneutical problems may frequently be insoluble in principle.

Where theology is concerned, perhaps we could say that the publication of Troeltsch's essay on the *Absoluteness of Christianity*[15] symbolized the beginning of the shift from ethnocentricity

12 P. Winch, *The Idea of a Social Science and its Relation to Philosophy* (London, 1958).
13 Needham, op. cit., p. 244.
14 M. Hesse, *In Defence of Objectivity* (London, 1972), p. 7 (reprinted from the Proceedings of the British Academy, lviii).
15 Tr. D. Read (London, 1972). The original lecture was delivered in 1901.

to relativism. However, the subsequent history of both
Catholic and Protestant theology has been marked by valiant
rearguard actions, resisting the further implications of that
shift. In order to set those battles in perspective it is, I believe,
important to remind ourselves that not only did Catholic
Modernism and Liberal Protestantism have more in common
than was realized by the exponents of either, but so also did
the official Catholic rejection of Modernism and the neo-
orthodox Protestant rejection of Liberalism (not that either
Pope Pius X or Karl Barth would necessarily be grateful for
the comparison).

Both Liberalism and Modernism felt the tension between
an affirmation of the eternal, imperishable significance and
validity of the truth disclosed in Jesus Christ and a
wholehearted acceptance of the contingency and particularity
of all historical truth. Both of them believed that they were
meeting that challenge, but the manner in which they did so
amounted, as their twentieth-century critics were not slow to
point out, to an evasion. Liberalism tended to drive a wedge
between 'historical' and 'religious' truth,[16] and to assume that
the 'essence' of Christianity may readily be discerned by employing the techniques of historical scholarship. Modernism
assumed that the forms adopted by Christianity in the course
of its history could be shown, by using the same critical historical techniques, to be successive faithful forms of Christian
truth.[17] The hermeneutical *naïveté* of both traditions led them
into an historical relativism from the standpoint of which
appeals to the abiding authority of the New Testament could
have little more than rhetorical value. But did their critics
meet the challenge any more successfully?

It can, I believe, be argued that both Barthian neo-
orthodoxy and Bultmannian existentialism also evaded, in the
last resort, the challenge which our critical historical consciousness poses for a faith whose truth-claims are inextricably

16 A tendency the roots of which can be traced back as far as Lessing: cf.
    W. Pannenberg, *Basic Questions in Theology, Vol. I* (London, 1970), p. 58.
17 Here, of course, I have principally Loisy in mind.

bound up with the exposed contingency of particular historical events.[18] Similary, it has been persuasively argued that
Tillich's attempt to hold together 'the claim that the foundation of Christian faith is historical and the claim that that
foundation is in principle unfalsifiable',[19] did not, in the last
analysis, succeed. Thus, according to Van Harvey, neither
Barth, Bultmann nor Tillich 'makes clear how it is possible to
be both a critical historian and a believer'.[20]

In theology, as in the other human sciences, it is becoming
increasingly generally acknowledged that, where problems of
interpretation are concerned, our starting-point today has to
be a willingness to accept the fact that the stranger *is* a
stranger. It is this acceptance, I suggest, which is lacking in
the work even of such massive, and massively influential
theologians as Barth and Bultmann. Thus Pannenberg, following Gadamer, denies Bultmann's 'presupposition of a
common self-understanding between the author and the
reader', and insists that 'Interpretation must first of all accept
the strangeness of the text'.[21]

So far as Catholic theology is concerned, the theories of
'doctrinal development' which flourished during the first half
of this century represented the theoretical component of the
initial Catholic response to that deepening sense of historicity,
of reality as process, which was a distinctive feature of
nineteenth-century consciousness. I should wish to argue that
these theories have, in the long run, turned out to be as inadequate a response as were the parallel developments in Protestant theology during the same period, and for not dissimilar
reasons. (A few years ago, Edward Schillebeeckx drew atten-

18 Cf. V. A. Harvey, *The Historian and the Believer* (London, 1967), p. 104; H.
     Zahrnt, *The Question of God* (London, 1969), pp. 243–4.
19 J. P. Clayton, 'Is Jesus Necessary for Christology? An Antinomy in
     Tillich's Theological Method', *Christ, Faith and History,* ed. S. W. Sykes
     and J. P. Clayton (Cambridge, 1972), p. 154.
20 Harvey, op. cit., p. 164.
21 G. Turner, 'Wolfhart Pannenberg and the Hermeneutical Problem',
     Irish Theological Quarterly, xxxix (1972), p. 115. Cf. H.–G. Gadamer,
     Truth and Method (London, 1975).

tion to this similarity, pointing out that discussion of the 'development of dogma' sprang from an awareness of the fact that, 'We cannot grasp the biblical text directly "in itself", as though we, as readers or believers, *transcended time'*. Hence, he went on, the problem 'presented thematically ... in terms of the "development of dogma" ... is the Catholic counterpart of what is known in Protestant theology as the "hermeneutical" problem'.[22])

The basic weakness of the two main groups of 'theories of doctrinal development' may be briefly indicated as follows.[23] If our affirmation of the continuity of belief and doctrine across the manifest discontinuities of Christian history rests, ultimately, upon an unconvincingly abstract conception of the history of ideas (which was the characteristic of so-called 'logical' theories of development); or if it rests upon an unhistorical conception of 'magisterium', which somehow places authoritative Church teaching outside the ebb and flow and variation of our cultural history (which was the characteristic of so-called 'theological' theories), then we are still seeking an illegitimate *immunity* from the risk, darkness and uncertainty that are endemic to our historically constituted condition.

I believe that the fundamental weakness of the Protestant and Catholic 'rearguard actions' can be quite briefly expressed. A 'high' theology of Scripture as the Word of God does not, cannot, make it easier to *understand* the biblical texts than would be the case if they were 'merely' the words of man. Similarly, a 'high' theology of the providential guidance of the Church in history by the Spirit of truth cannot make it easier to show *how* contemporary beliefs and doctrines are faithful to the original message, than would be the case if we had to do with a 'merely human' history. The official Catholic rejection of Modernism, and the neo-orthodox Protestant rejection of nineteenth-century Liberalism, were both born out of a concern effectively to affirm the eternal, imperishable significance

22 E. Schillebeeckx, *God the Future of Man*, tr. N. D. Smith (London, 1969), p. 6.
23 Cf. N. L. A. Lash, *Change in Focus* (London, 1973), pp. 119–27.

of the truth disclosed in Jesus Christ. But, in both cases, the forms in which that concern was expressed were such as fundamentally to evade the problems posed for Christian belief by a deepening historical consciousness.

In recent years, the emergence of the 'New Quest', Pannenberg's critique of Barth, and the mounting dissatisfaction expressed with 'theories of doctrinal development', may be taken as indices of an increasing recognition of the profound gulf which separates the biblical authors from ourselves, and of the fact that we may neither simply 'leap across' this gulf, nor bridge it with fragile structures of abstract theory. As historical discontinuity becomes a central, and no longer a peripheral issue; as we become more conscious of the social, contextual determination of the consciousness and language of both the interpreter and of the author whom he seeks to understand; as cultural pluralism generates an ever more radical theological pluralism; we find ourselves haunted by the question which, as we saw a little earlier, today dictates the concerns of other human sciences, namely: Can we understand a stranger?

From Colonialism to Dialogue
It is important not to have any illusions as to what is at stake. If we conclude, as some contemporary philosophers of science would conclude, that we cannot *in principle* understand the stranger, then we are forced to accept an agnostic relativism in which truth is determined, not by the world, but by the postulates of theory. The consequences for ethical theory, and for a theology which wishes to maintain that a Word once spoken, in a context very different from our own, is of imperishable validity, hardly need to be spelt out. And the position would be little better if we decided that, although it was possible in principle to understand the stranger, it was rarely if ever possible in practice.

It is tempting to appeal to the concept of 'human nature' as a way out of our difficulty. Thus, according to Rickman,

Dilthey's answer to the question as to the possibility of historical knowledge may be summarized as follows: 'human minds can understand history because they are dealing with what other human minds have created'.[24] And Bernard Lonergan's notion of 'transcendental method', resting upon an assumption of the fundamental invariance of human cognitional structures across cultural change, enables him to argue that the recognition of a variety of distinct contexts of meaning does not render the task of transcultural interpretation impossible.

Now it must be admitted that an insistence on the fundamentally nonrevisable and culturally invariant cognitional structure of the human subject is of more than trivial significance. Were it not the case that we are entitled to trust in this, our persistent attempts to understand would have no rational basis. If there were no common constituent features shared by the cognitional structure and performance of all those whom we recognize as human subjects, our classification of those subjects *as* human would be meaningless. As Wittgenstein said, if a lion spoke, we would not understand him.

Nevertheless, there is a serious weakness in an appeal, such as Lonergan's, to formally invariant cognitional structures. Such an appeal tells us nothing about *how* particular individuals, members of particular societies, go about the business of being attentive, intelligent, reasonable, and responsible.[25] Needham may be overstating the case, but he is nonetheless making a point of considerable importance, when he says that 'the question whether man's reasoning is or is not everywhere the same can be decided only by comparative ethnography'.[26]

In other words, while an appeal to a fundamentally invariant human nature may be a justified heuristic device, warranting the rationality of the ongoing hermeneutical quest,

24 H. P. Rickman, ed., *Meaning in History. W. Dilthey's Thoughts on History and Society* (London, 1961), p. 64.
25 Cf. N. L. A. Lash, 'Method and Cultural Discontinuity', *Looking at Lonergan's Method,* pp. 127–43.
26 Needham, op. cit., p. 159.

it does not help us, in practice, to overcome problems of interpretation generated by the recognition of discontinuity between significantly different linguistic and cultural contexts.

We must look elsewhere. As a first clue indicating the direction in which we might look, I would like to draw the reader's attention to a rather obvious fact. All the authors and movements so far mentioned stemmed from Western Europe or North America. A hundred years ago, still riding the crest of colonial and missionary expansion, the white man knew that he was the centre of the universe of meaning. More specifically, the educated, middle-class or bourgeois white man knew what was good for the black man or the working man, for the 'lower orders' or for Kipling's 'lesser breeds without the law'. The European intellectual had an unruffled confidence in the normativity of the cognitional procedures characteristic of his ethnic and social milieu. Today, the universe of meaning has no centre. That universe has been decentred by the erosion of assumptions of inherited or God-given superiority. In so far as an individual, or a group, experience other individuals or groups as equals, they are also thereby experienced precisely as 'other'. Once the assumption that the stranger is inferior is shattered, then he is experienced as a stranger. And once you admit that you do not understand him, you are gradually forced to admit that you do not understand yourself.

In the encounter with the stranger, he is experienced as a potential threat, and a potential partner. We are obliged to choose between treating him as an enemy or as a friend. If we decide to treat him as an enemy, as one who threatens our self-understanding and identity, then the only way in which we can 'understand' him, can comprehend him, is either by destroying him or by assimilating him. And assimilation is itself a form of destruction: it negates his particularity, his otherness. (I am suggesting, in other words, that ethnocentricity is the hermeneutical dimension of colonialism.)

If, on the other hand, we decide to treat him as a friend, as a potential partner, then we are taking the risk of having *our* self-understanding radically transformed. And not only our self-understanding, but also those economic, social and political patterns and structures of which our beliefs and attitudes are the conscious dimension.

It could be objected that, in the last few paragraphs, my argument has degenerated into metaphorical allusion, with all its attendant imprecision. But I wanted to do three things.

Firstly, by appealing to our everyday experience of interpersonal relations, I wanted to suggest that there is an ethical dimension to the task of interpretation. This should come as no great surprise to us, as Christians, who affirm that it is sin that divides men, that sets apart as strangers those created to be brothers, and that it is the redemptive grace of God which transforms strangers into brethren. As John MacMurray put it: 'My knowledge of another person is a function of my love for him.'[27]

This insistence that hermeneutical success, or epistemological success in general, presupposes, as a necessary condition, the risk and venture of trust, of love, is no new suggestion. It is one of the most striking characteristics of Newman's thought, especially in the *University Sermons*.

But, secondly, to say that there is an ethical dimension to the task of interpretation is, by implication, to question the primacy of the theoretical. Raymond Williams has remarked that: 'The most difficult thing to get hold of, in studying any past period, is the felt sense of the quality of life at a particular place and time: a sense of the ways in which the particular activities combined into a way of thinking and living. . . . The term I would suggest to describe it is a *structure of feeling*. . . . In one sense, this structure of feeling is the culture of a period: it is the particular living result of all the elements in the general organisation.'[28]

If our encounter with the stranger calls in question our self-understanding, it thereby calls in question that structure

27 J. MacMurray, *Persons in Relation* (London, 1961), p. 170.
28 R. Williams, *The Long Revolution* (London, Penguin Books, 1965), pp. 63–4.

of feeling, that culture, of which our theoretical attitudes and positions are a secondary and derivative expression. And if, in order to understand the stranger whom we have decided to love, we discover that we are being challenged to restructure our culture, our structure of feeling, this transformation cannot take place in the imagination alone: it must take place in fact. It is in this sense that the acknowledgement of the ethical dimension of the task of interpretation entails questioning the primacy of the theoretical. And once again, this emphasis on the primacy of action is no new suggestion. According to MacMurray, it goes back to Kant.[29] It certainly goes back to Marx and, along another line, through Blondel to Newman's view of the relationship between notional and real apprehension and assent.

It follows from this that there is what we might call an organizational dimension to the task of interpretation. I have already indicated this, but it may be worth approaching it from a slightly different angle. The 'lived culture' of a particular time and place is never wholly accessible to, wholly recoverable in, another context of meaning.[30] It is impossible to translate without remainder. But, in order to understand, as adequately as possible, an alien 'structure of feeling', it is necessary to discover the aims and intentions of which the stranger's beliefs and commitments were the embodiment or expression. To quote MacMurray again: 'Historical understanding is . . . a comprehension of the continuity of human intention.'[31] Now, human intentions are expressed and embodied not only in beliefs and statements, but also in the forms of organization which men create in pursuit of the goals which they intend. Therefore, to say that the encounter with the stranger calls in question our self-understanding is to say

---

29 'As Kant rightly concluded, it is the practical that is primary. The theoretical is secondary and derivative', J. MacMurray, *The Self as Agent* (London, 1957), p. 81. This theme runs throughout these early chapters on Kant.

30 Cf. Williams, op. cit., p. 66.

31 MacMurray, *The Self as Agent*, p. 213.

that it calls in question those organizational patterns in which our present self-understanding is embodied.

In the third place, it might be objected that, to offer the model of interpersonal relations as a basis for hermeneutical theory, in the way that I have done, is to abandon all concern for objectivity. It could be argued (as it is argued, for example, in Roger Trigg's little book, *Reason and Commitment*[32]) that to give priority to love, to trust, to action, to commitment, is to start down the slippery slope alone which rationality, objectivity and – eventually – truth are abandoned.

But such an objection rests upon a crude empiricist notion of objectivity which is being increasingly rejected by those very natural sciences which originally gave it birth. Mary Hesse, in the British Academy lecture to which I referred earlier, has suggested that Habermas' model of hermeneutics as dialogue is of interest, not only in the philosophy of the human sciences (to which Habermas restricts it), but also in the philosophy of the natural sciences. 'The guarantee of objectivity in human science is the participation in *dialogue* between investigator and investigated, in which *reciprocal* interaction occurs. The sanction of failure is disturbance of consensus and breakdown of communication.'[33] And she goes on: 'For a historian operating according to this model, neither the anachronistic reconstruction of past science in the light of modern theories and modern evidence, nor the deliberate suppression of these in the attempt to become a "seventeenth-century man", are satisfactory or indeed possible. What is required is a sympathetic attempt to enter into seventeenth-century thought forms and problems *without* abandonment of the criteria provided by subsequent developments.'[34]

32 Cambridge, 1973.
33 Hesse, op. cit., p. 14.
34 Ibid., p. 15.

Questions in Conclusion

By way of conclusion, I would now like briefly to consider three rather obvious objections to the way in which I have been working in this paper.

In the first place, does not the model of 'dialogue' with a 'stranger' (a model some features of which have characterised classical hermeneutical theory from Dilthey to Gadamer and Habermas) confusingly gloss over a fundamental difference between, say, anthropology and sociology on the one hand, and historical understanding on the other? The difference that I have in mind can be pinpointed by drawing attention to the obvious fact that the dead cannot answer back.

It is important not to underestimate the significance of this difference, one implication of which is that, as applied to forms of historical knowledge, the status of the model is more clearly metaphorical. It may, nevertheless, still be the case that the methodology of the social sciences can illuminate problems of historical hermeneutic in ways such as those that I have tried to indicate.

In the second place, have I not overstated the difficulty of understanding the stranger? I do not think so. The depth of mutual incomprehension between individuals, and between groups of human beings, hardly needs arguing for: the evidence is there, from the divorce courts to the gas chamber; from racial tensions in Bradford to the bloodstained battle-fields of world history. I have been arguing that it is insufficient merely to assert, abstractly, that men can 'in principle'. understand each other. It is incumbent upon hermeneutical practice *and theory* to indicate how, in fact, they may be enabled to do so. In other words, questions concerning the possibility of understanding the stranger are 'practical' questions in the sense, combinative of non-dialectical concepts of both theory and practice, in which Marx uses the term in the second 'Thesis on Feuerbach'.[35]

35 'The question whether truth can be attributed to human thinking is not a question of theory but is a *practical* question. Man must prove the truth, i.e. the reality and power, the this-sidedness of his thinking in

In the third place, are not some of my tentative positive suggestions manifestly ridiculous: how can social and political change, for example, possibly be a precondition for understanding the New Testament? If one accepts (as classical hermeneutical theory seems to do) that good interpretation changes the interpreter, the question that needs to be asked is: Who is the interpreter? Is he not an element in that 'structure of feeling' which constitutes his culture? And if he is, then to affirm that he can be called in question and transformed without calling in question and transforming the culture of which he forms a part seems to entail subscription to a discredited individualism.

In this paper I have cast my net disgracefully wide, dragging in a whole shoal of issues each of which would need at least a paper on its own for its adequate exploration. I have done so not, I think, out of any predilection for eclectic dilettantism, but rather because I believe that there is, by now, ample evidence that certain crucial methodological problems in theology, in the social sciences, and in the history and philosophy of the natural sciences, exhibit sufficient common features to recommend their common, or at least their collaborative exploration in the search for a solution.

---

practice. The dispute over the reality or non-reality of thinking that is isolated from practice is a purely *scholastic* question', K. Marx, *Early Writings* (London, Pelican Marx Library, 1975), p. 422.

5. SHOULD CHRISTIANITY BE CREDIBLE?

This paper is entitled 'Should Christianity be Credible?' rather than 'Is Christianity Credible?' because the answer to the latter question is, on at least one level, quite simply 'Yes'.[1] Millions of men and women continue to find Christianity credible, continue to draw inspiration and guidance for their life and understanding from the Gospel, and from at least some features of that which two thousand years of action and reflection have made of the Gospel. But the suspicion lurks that these people only continue to find Christianity credible because they lack the courage, the intelligence or the information to admit or to perceive that the characteristic claims of Christian belief have been rendered ever more untenable by social, political and intellectual developments in the modern world. And this may help to explain why it is to theologians that the question has been addressed. After all, however lamentably defective the faith, prayer and practice of the theologian, he is supposed to be someone who is *intellectually* alive to the problems that attend any serious consideration of the extent to which Christianity 'ought' still to be credible in our time and place.

There are a number of reasons that I can think of for ceasing to be a Christian. The apparent fragility of the historical component of the grounds of Christian belief: there is much

---

1   This article was first published, as the second in a series of responses by theologians to the question: 'Is Christianity Credible?', in the *Epworth Review*, v (1978), pp. 76–81.

less that we can confidently claim to know of Jesus of Nazareth, his words and work, his message and his fate, than once seemed to be the case. The impossibility of speaking simply about 'God' without laying oneself open to the suspicion that one is naively evading the cluster of critical questions – logical, philosophical, ethical and sociological – that have, in recent centuries, been put to all religious discourse, at least in so far as such discourse purports to make true statements that are not reducible to statements about human attitudes, hopes and fears. The willingness of many Christian theologians to withdraw from the public places in our culture where the quest for resolution or illumination of the mystery of human existence is pursued (is it possible to attribute *simply* to ignorance and fashionable prejudice the current tendency to describe as 'merely theological' any argument that is manifestly an exercise in trivial, freewheeling irrelevance?). The poverty (and sometimes worse) of our response, at both the practical and the theoretical levels, to questions of economics and genetics, ecology and sexuality, revolution and starvation, peace and freedom.

I do not, therefore, find it surprising that, for many people, the claims of Christian belief and, centrally, the claim that 'God was in Christ, reconciling the world to himself', seem to have been deprived of their warrants, coherence, significance and plausibility. Nor do I find it surprising that there are other people who cling to their Christian belief as something which provides them with a bulwark against panic and despair, a still point of personal and emotional security in a world of terrifyingly complex confusion, hostility and unmeaning. I have in mind those Christians whose faith, grounded in appeals to deeply personal experience of grace and assurance, is insulated (by any one of a number of intellectual devices) from historical, philosophical, ethical or social criticism.

And yet, if I found myself unable to continue to confess the Christian faith, unable to continue to affirm that 'God was in Christ, reconciling the world to himself', I hope that I would have the courage to take the former route, into agnosticism or 'practical atheism', rather than the latter. There are a number of reasons for this.

In the first place, I am profoundly suspicious of what I might call 'methodological schizophrenia', of a refusal continually to seek for connections, both practical and theoretical, between all aspects of our experience – personal, social, intellectual, emotional, sexual, political, historical, scientific – and between the various levels and types of discourse in which those aspects find expression. Nor is this, I think, simply a matter of temperament. As I read the history of Jewish and Christian belief and practice, I am forced to the conclusion that any restriction of the significance of Christian faith to some and only some aspects of human experience and behaviour is an impoverishment and a betrayal of the original message. There are a number of ways of putting this. If the concept of 'religion', or of 'religious experience', is taken to refer exclusively to some particular feature or aspect of human experience, behaviour and language, then, as I understand it, Christianity is not adequately characterized as a 'religion'. Or again: the God of Christian belief is confessed to be creator as well as redeemer; he is the Lord of history and the Lord of the world. And my faith in him has consequences for the way I act in respect of, and seek to understand, not simply my personal history and ultimate destiny, but every event in history and every feature of the furniture of the world. Or again: the confession that 'God was in Christ, reconciling the world to himself' is to be construed as saying something, not only about God and man, but also about the way the *world* was, is and will be.

But there is a second, perhaps more fundamental, reason why I regard the agnostic option as preferable to that form of pietism that I indicated earlier. Undoubtedly we all need security, we 'cannot bear very much reality'. Nevertheless, I have a horror of illusion. Whenever, in theological discussion, I hear considerations of 'meaningfulness' or 'relevance' being given greater weight than considerations of truth, I get suspicious. I am a physical coward, but I hope that I might be given the courage to die for that which I believed to be true. I could certainly *not* die for that which I merely found 'meaningful' or 'relevant'.

Wolfhart Pannenberg has said that 'the most fundamental question which can face a man' is: 'In what do we ultimately put our trust? What are our hearts set on, in the last resort?'[2] I have been invited to indicate why it is that I continue to seek ultimately to put my trust in the reality and promise of the God who raises Jesus from the dead, and what it is that I understand myself to be doing in thus expressing, in the confession of Christian faith, the character and object of this ultimate trust. But there is more to Pannenberg's question than that. I have already spoken of the danger of illusion. The person who declares that he puts his ultimate trust in the God of Christian belief is taking a twofold series of risks. On the one hand, there is the series of risks to which, at the academic level, it is the business of historians, New Testament scholars and philosophers of religion to attend. Thus, for example, there is the risk that to speak of God is to speak of that to which there is nothing that corresponds in reality except those social expectations and constraints which we project, as it were, onto a metaphysical screen; the risk that God is made in our image and likeness, is a product of our imagination. There is also the risk that we have misunderstood the fact and significance of Jesus of Nazareth. Put these together, and there is the risk that there is not God, and therefore it is not and cannot be the case that 'God was in Christ, reconciling the world to himself'.

On the other hand, there is the quite different series of risks attendant upon our capacity to fool ourselves. 'What our hearts are really set on', says Pannenberg, 'can be very different from what we say or think is of prime importance to us.'[3] I may believe, in all sincerity, that my trust is ultimately put in the God and Father of our Lord Jesus Christ. And I may be

---

2   W. Pannenberg, *The Apostles' Creed in the Light of Today's Questions* (London, 1972), p. 4.

3   Loc. cit.

wrong. Sometimes this can become apparent from my actions, sometimes it can be uncovered by psychological or sociological scrutiny. But, more usually, the truth of the matter is in large measure veiled both from ourselves and from other people. And if this second series of risks can, no more than the first, ever be entirely guarded against, at least we can be prudent: we can attempt that measure of individual and corporate critical self-awareness that exposes the cruder contradictions between theory and practice, between what makes us tick and what we unreflectively suppose makes us tick.

In both the previous two paragraphs I have had at the back of my mind certain features of the Marxist critique of religion, features which present a challenge to Christian believing of which much English theology – even when it supposes itself to be 'radical' – often seems disturbingly unaware. In order to indicate some of the issues at stake, it may help briefly to consider the question: in what sense can or should a Christian believer be a 'materialist'?

Outrageously to oversimplify complex and controverted issues, it can, I think, be said that Marxist 'materialism' (which, it must be remembered, defined itself in contrast – at least in part – to Hegelian 'idealism' as interpreted by Marx) expresses the conviction that you cannot change the world merely by changing the way in which you think about it and speak about it. 'Once upon a time', wrote Marx in a famous parable, 'a valiant fellow had the idea that men were drowned in water only because they were possessed with the idea of gravity.'[4] If you say to a Marxist that you are not a materialist, that you believe in the primacy of the spirit, he will probably take you to mean that you suffer from the illusion that, if only we could knock the silly idea of gravity out of people's heads, they would, as Marx put it, be 'sublimely proof against any danger from water'.[5]

---

4   K. Marx and F. Engels, *The German Ideology* (London, Lawrence and Wishart, 1974), p. 37.
5   Loc. cit.

Some theologians, describing Christian belief as an 'interpretation of reality', a 'way of looking at things', sometimes leave me with the uneasy feeling that they suppose that, if only we could knock the silly idea of atheism out of people's heads, they would be better off. But would they? Is it absolutely certain that to interpret the world *as it is* as the expression of God's love is preferable to interpreting it atheistically? Might not an interpretation in Christian terms, which left the world as it is, be merely a palliative, a drug, rendering the intolerable tolerable? Marx certainly thought so and, as an atheist, he therefore thought it important that the palliating illusion should wither and die so that, confronting the reality of the situation, we might be motivated and stimulated to do whatever is in our power to change it.

But may not a Christian believer, for whom the action of God is affirmed to be ultimate reality, not comforting illusion, nevertheless agree with the Marxist that to encourage people to 'see things differently', while leaving things as they are, is to reinforce their slavery, the reinforcement being all the more insidious in that it is presented as the proclamation of the truth that sets us free?

The Marxist critique can, I suggest, only be met if we hold our Christian faith as the entitlement and enablement to *act*, to enter co-operatively into the work of a God who has acted, acts and will act to set men free, and not simply as a way of 'regarding', 'looking at' or 'interpreting' reality. The manner of our action demands expression: we seek to give an account of the hope that is in us. Christianity, as practice, has its interpretative 'moment'. I have already suggested that Christian belief, as I understand it, stands or falls on the question of truth. Nevertheless, for reasons that have, I hope, now become clear, I regard Professor Peter Baelz's claim that 'Christianity is first and foremost a conviction and a belief, and that a Christian style of life is a response to this belief'[6] as, at best,

---

6   P. R. Baelz, 'Is Christianity Credible?', *Epworth Review*, iv (1977), p. 67. Baelz acknowledges that 'living, doing, responding are somehow more basic than mere believing' (loc. cit.). The ambiguity arises because,

ambiguous and, at worst, an unintended encouragement of
the 'idealism' that continues to threaten contemporary patterns of Christian speech and behaviour.

People are not saved from drowning by thinking differently
about the law of gravity. People are not saved by thinking
differently about the 'laws' of human history and human destiny. People are saved from drowning as a result of certain
changes being brought about in their concrete, objective situation (by somebody dragging them from the water, for
example). People are saved – from sin, from death, from the
ultimacy of chaos – if the deepest reality and definitive outcome of human existence is, in fact, a state of affairs that is
appropriately spoken of in terms of the effective victory of love,
of life, of freedom. How things have been, are and will be is
more important than how we think things have been, are and
will be. In other words, however unfashionable an 'objective'
account of atonement may be, and however difficult it may be
to find the language that can give appropriate expression to
such an account, it is fundamental to the manner in which I
hold my Christian beliefs that the affirmation that 'God was in
Christ, reconciling the world to himself' is understood to say
something about what is in fact the case independently of my
recognition that it is the case. Not that such recognition is
unimportant for, if what is in fact the case is appropriately to
be declared to be the case, then the truth of the affirmation
must 'show itself' in the work of reconciliation.

Should Christianity be credible? Only to the extent that it
succeeds in meeting, both practically and theoretically, the
challenges that are put to it. So far, I have done little more
than suggest what some of these challenges are, and to affirm
that I seek to be and to remain a Christian, someone whose
ultimate trust is put in the reality and promise of the God and
Father of our Lord Jesus Christ. Is it possible, by way of

---

when he says that Christianity is 'first and foremost ... a belief', he is
in fact considering, not the relation between theory and practice, but
rather that between two sets of 'beliefs': between 'what a Christian
believes to be the case' and 'how he considers he ought to act' (loc. cit.).

conclusion, briefly to indicate what it would be that would erode that trust, obliging me to withdraw the affirmation that the claims of Christian belief are, fundamentally, true?

It is not too difficult to indicate the outline of the sort of answer that can be given, in the abstract, to such a question. Thus, for example, if I were to become convinced that Jesus did not exist, or that the story told in the New Testament of his life, teaching and death was a fictional construction ungrounded in the facts, or a radical *mis*interpretation of his character, history and significance, then I should cease to be a Christian. If I were to become convinced, not simply that my image and understanding of God was shaped and influenced by the cultural milieu of which I am a product (for this will always be the case; hence the continual need for 'negative theology', for the eloquent silence of the mystics, correcting and purifying the perennial tendency of anthropomorphism to slide into idolatry) but that Feuerbach was right, and that to speak of God was *simply* an ornamental and indirect way of speaking of man, then I should cease to be a Christian. If the manner in which the Christian community proclaimed and celebrated and sought to embody the Gospel seemed more evidently and persistently (whatever its admirable intentions and 'religious' self-consciousness) to reinforce human slavery than to foster human freedom, then I should cease to be a Christian.

But that is simply an outline of the sort of answer that can be given, in the abstract, to the question that I raised. In the concrete, the answer would take shape rather differently. Our central, concrete convictions and commitments – in marriage, in politics, in religion – are such that, against them, 'nothing counts simply'.[7] We grow into love with another person from an accumulation of innumerable events, perceptions and circumstances. We do not say: 'Tomorrow, I will take the leap into a relationship of love and commitment to X.' Rather we

7   J. Coulson, 'Belief and Imagination', *Downside Review*, xc (1972), p. 10. Coulson is discussing Newman's treatment of 'certitude' which, throughout this and the following paragraph, I have in mind.

discover, looking over our shoulder, as it were, that we have come to be in love with another person, that the certitude of conviction and commitment has been grown into by a process the logic of which defies formal expression. And the erosion of the relationship is a process as complex and (usually) as gradual as the process of its construction.

Something similar is the case with political and religious conviction. Against deeply held political and religious beliefs, nothing counts simply. We grow into political or religious certitude. We do not say: 'Today I am a Tory (or an apolitical animal); tomorrow I shall be a convinced socialist.' And, where religious certitude is concerned, most talk of the 'leap of faith' is similarly ridiculous. Conviction is not leapt into. The discovery that we have come to hold a certain set of beliefs may be sudden but, on reflection, we can usually see something of the complexity of the process whereby those beliefs were cumulatively, slowly and often painfully acquired. And the erosion of political or religious conviction is a process as complex and (usually) as gradual as the process of its acquisition.

In principle, therefore, there can be no way of guaranteeing that I shall not, one day, discover that I have ceased to be a Christian. And should that day arrive, I hope I should have the courage and integrity to admit the fact. In practice, it would seem that it is in prayer and the 'common life of the body of Christ', more fundamentally than in the quest for theoretical or historical certainty, that the sustaining and deepening of Christian conviction is to be sought. And if the trustfulness of faith is, in the life of every Christian (and not only of the professional theologian) set in permanent tension with the critical questing and testing of theological reflection, there is no reason to suppose that such tension is necessarily destructive, rather than constitutive, of our many-sided journey into truth.

PART THREE:
APPROACHES TO THEOLOGY

When we speak of theological 'pluralism' we refer, not only to a variety of things believed, models employed, images preferred but – more fundamentally – to a variety of methods, of theological approaches. As I have already indicated in the Introduction, my own approach differs significantly from that adopted by Professor Maurice Wiles. He now turns up again, this time in company with Professor Hans Küng: in very different ways, they illustrate something of the variety of contemporary approaches to the work of the theologian (Chapters Seven and Eight). And because I have learned a great deal in these matters from John Henry Newman, it seemed a good idea to include a discussion of a key text in which Newman discusses the work of the theologian and its relationship to other aspects of Christian belief, life and organisation (Chapter Six).

6. LIFE, LANGUAGE AND ORGANIZATION: ASPECTS OF THE THEOLOGICAL MINISTRY[1]

Newman's last major work was the essay with which, in 1877, he prefaced the third edition of his *Via Media of the Anglican Church*. In the introduction to his study of this Preface Professor Richard Bergeron, having sketched that tripolar dialectic of functions in which Newman describes the life of a community that is 'at once a philosophy, a political power and a religious rite',[2] goes on to say that, if the action of the Church were only regulated by the principle specific to each function, then the unity of the Church would be seriously threatened, because these principles pull the ecclesial body in divergent if not opposed directions. It is therefore necessary to discover higher rules ('règles supérieures') capable of maintaining the balance of the whole and of orienting the action of the Church in a direction which guarantees the common good while respecting the exigencies of each function.[3] There are, he says, two such higher rules or 'regulating principles': 'la juridiction universelle de la théologie et la divine économie'.[4]

So far as the second of these is concerned, it is undoubtedly the case that the 'principle of economy' is what this Preface is

1 Originally delivered at an International Newman Congress held in Freiburg-im-Breisgau in 1978, this paper is also scheduled for publication in a forthcoming volume of *Newman-Studien*.
2 J. H. Newman, *The Via Media of the Anglican Church, I* (³London, 1877), p. xl. *(V.M.I)*.
3 Cf. R. Bergeron, *Les Abus de l'Eglise d'Après Newman* (Paris, 1971), pp. 17, 107.
4 Bergeron, p. 107.

primarily all about. Only by an appeal to this principle, and an indication of the way in which it operates in practice, can Newman answer the charge which, as an Anglican, he had levelled against the Catholic Church: namely, that the Church's deeds fatally contradicted its words, that its practice was inconsistent with its theory.[5]

It is also true that, in this Preface, Newman does indeed describe 'Theology' as 'the fundamental and regulating principle of the whole Church system'.[6] John Coulson, whose analysis of the Preface is very similar to Bergeron's, says that 'theology is singled out as having the authority of the prophetical office to act as the equilibrating principle'.[7] For both Coulson and Bergeron, it is in the isolation of this need for a 'regulative principle', and in the recognition that it is theology, rather than, for example, religious experience or church order, which must exercise this 'equilibrating' authority, that the genius, originality and abiding significance of the Preface are above all to be discerned.

This is an attractive interpretation, and one for which there is ample warrant in Newman's texts (but then it can be said of Newman, as B. H. Streeter said of the Fathers, that you can prove anything from his writings provided only that your edition has a good index and that you do not look up all the references). It is, however, perhaps a little too attractive, a little too convenient, especially for those of us who exercise a theological ministry in a Church which is only slowly, and not without pain and confusion, rediscovering the necessity of ascribing to that ministry a function and an authority irreducibly distinct, in principle if not necessarily in practice, from the function and authority of episcopal office.

We might put it this way. On Newman's account, the three offices frequently, and inevitably, find themselves set on collision courses. However, if we bear in mind Newman's remark, at the end of the Preface, that 'whatever is great refuses to be

5 Cf. *V.M.I.* pp. xxxvii–xxxviii.
6 *V.M.I*, p. xlvii.
7 J. Coulson, *Newman and the Common Tradition* (Oxford, 1970), p. 167.

reduced to human rule, and to be made consistent in its many aspects with itself',[8] we should not, I believe, suppose the conflictual relationship between the three offices to be necessarily capable of theoretical resolution. Thus, for example, the theologian, wearied by the struggle, may not console himself by having recourse to the claim that, after all, it is *'theology* which is singled out as having the authority of the prophetical office to act as the equilibrating principle'. It is fundamental to the phenomenological analysis of the Preface, and to its apologetic concerns, that no one of the 'offices' may claim immunity from regulation by the others: 'each has to find room for the claims of the other two'.[9] For too long, in Catholic Christianity, the 'regal office' has claimed just such immunity, thus usurping, as Newman came to see with increasing clarity, the rights of the 'priestly' and 'prophetical' offices. And Protestant Christianity, from the eighteenth century to the present day, has been marked by the struggle for supremacy between 'experience' and 'argument', between 'pietism' and 'rationalism', between the 'priestly' and 'prophetical' offices. And yet, I repeat, the greatness of the Preface consists in Newman's refusal to allocate to any one of the three offices a position of privilege or centrality in respect of the others.

But what are we then to make of Newman's explicit assertion that 'Theology is the fundamental and regulating principle of the whole Church system'?[10] I want to suggest that there is an ambiguity in the argument of the section in which that assertion occurs. Before discussing the passage in any detail I shall, firstly, comment on some earlier formulations of the 'triadic' character of Christian existence and, secondly, draw attention to the context in which the notion of a 'regulating principle' makes its appearance, in the *Grammar of Assent.* Having concentrated, for most of this paper, on the relationship between the 'prophetical' and 'priestly' offices I shall, in a

8 *V.M.I,* p. xciv.
9 *V.M.I,* p. xli.
10 *V.M.I,* p. xlvii

final section, make a few observations concerning the relationship between the 'prophetical' and 'regal' offices; more specifically, concerning the relationship between the theological ministry and ecclesiastical authority.

The reflection of the 'Three Offices of Christ' in the life and ministry of the Church, and of the individual Christian, was first explored by Newman in a sermon of that title preached in 1840.[11] There he suggested that Christ uniquely combines in his person and work 'the three principle conditions of mankind' (pp. 53–4). As one who 'performed the priest's service ... on the Cross' he represents 'one large class of men, or aspect of mankind ... that of sufferers, – such as slaves, the oppressed, the poor, the sick, the bereaved, the troubled in mind' (p. 54). As king, as the embodiment of God's rule, he represents 'those who work and toil, who are full of business and engagements, whether for themselves or for others' (p. 54). As prophet, he represents 'the studious, learned, and wise' (p. 54).

If, however, we reflect on the manner in which Christ combined 'such contrary modes of life, and their contrary excellence' (p. 55), we discover how radically the form of each has been reshaped by its coincidence with the others: 'He suffered, yet He triumphed. He was humble and despised, yet He was a teacher' (p. 54). In so far as the community of the Church and, indeed, each individual Christian – for 'all His followers in some sense bear all three offices' (p. 55) – conform to his 'pattern', the exercise of each office will be similarly, and paradoxically, transformed.

Consider, for example, what we might call the 'worldly' or unregenerate form of the prophetical office: the teacher without Christ. 'We know that philosophers of this world are men of deep reflection and inventive genius ... These are the men, who at length change the face of society, reverse laws and opinions, subvert governments, and overthrow kingdoms; or they extend the range of our knowledge, and, as it were,

11 J. H. Newman, *Sermons Bearing on Subjects of the Day* (London, 1869), pp. 52–62. On this sermon, cf. Bergeron, pp. 102–4; Coulson, p. 170. *(S.D.)*.

introduce us into new worlds. Well, this is admirable, surely, so vast is the power of mind; but observe how inferior is this display of intellectual greatness compared with that which is seen in Christ and His saints. . . . These great philosophers of the world, whose words are so good and so effective, are themselves too often nothing more than words. . . . They can sit at ease, and follow their own pleasure, and indulge the flesh, or serve the world, while their reason is so enlightened, and their words are so influential. Of all forms of earthly greatness, surely this is the most despicable?' (p. 60). He is, we remember, preaching in Oxford!

'Endurance, active life, thought – these are the three . . . principal states in which men find themselves' (p. 54). Therefore, 'Knowledge, power, endurance, are the three privileges of the Christian Church' (p. 56). But, through their unification in Christ, the character of each 'state' and each 'privilege' is radically transformed. Thus, for example, the mode of knowledge of the Christian – of every Christian and, *a fortiori,* of the theologian or 'Christian philosopher' – is of a knowledge born of endurance. The unregenerate philosopher, the thinker without Christ, as presented in the long passage that I have quoted (a passage which, in both irony and argument, foreshadows the sketch of the 'gentleman' in *The Idea of a University*[12]) is one of whom Newman asks: 'What shall we say to men like Balaam, who profess without doing, who teach the truth yet live in vice, who know, but do not love?'.[13]

Does it not follow, therefore, where the relationship between the prophetical and the priestly offices, between 'thought' and 'endurance' are concerned, that, if any position of primacy, any 'universal jurisdiction', is to be accorded to the prophetical office, it can only be such as to respect that primacy of the practical, the experiential, the concrete, which is the recurrent and central theme in Newman's philosophy of religion, from the *University Sermons* to the *Grammar of Assent?* The Christian

12 Cf. J. H. Newman, *The Idea of a University,* edited by I. T. Ker (Oxford, 1976), pp. 179–81.
13 *S.D.,* p. 61.

thinker, the thinker whose existence is patterned on the ministry of Christ, will not be a rationalist, or idealist, who supposes 'thought' to be autonomous and primary, albeit patent of 'application' in action and suffering. He will, in the terminology of this sermon, be one who thinks out of endurance, who reflects on action.

Before leaving this sermon, there is one other point that I should like to make. Coulson suggests that it is only as a result of his experience as a Roman Catholic that Newman discovered 'that the traditional application of the three offices of Christ to the Church was intended for more specific purposes than pastoral or liturgical rhetoric': namely, for the construction, in Mgr Nédoncelle's phrase, of 'une théologie des abus ecclésiastiques'.[14] As I read this sermon, however, it shows Newman already aware of how little the exercise of the three offices in the Church is, in fact, transformed by their unification in Christ. In other words, it already contains at least the seeds of that analysis of Christian distortions to which he will give more structured expression in the *Via Media* Preface.

The next passage on which I would like briefly to comment occurs in an entry, dated 24 January 1867, in the *Philosophical Notebook*. Here, the triad of 'endurance', 'action' and 'thought' appears as 'devotion' or 'passion', 'party adherence' or 'fellowship', and 'philosophy' or 'science'. With this shift in terminology he is, as it were, mid-way between the 1840 Sermon and the 1877 Preface. Here is the passage: '"Catholics"', he writes, still smarting from Kingsley, '"do not honestly seek truth". This misapprehension arises from the fact that religion is not solely a *philosophy* (science), but also a *devotion* (passion) and a party adherence or a fellowship. Devotion brings in hope and fear – and fellowship brings in fear of scandal. In philosophy there is no fear or consideration of any thing but "is this so or not?" but devotion brings in the fear of error and

14 Coulson, p. 170; cf. M. Nédoncelle, 'Newman, théologien des abus de l'Eglise', *Oecumenica 1967* (Neuchâtel, 1967), pp. 116–34. Coulson quotes the phrase from another essay of Nédoncelle's.

its consequences, and fellowship introduces the necessities of all moving together – the duty of deference to superiors, and consulting for the interest of our neighbours. N.B. All this must come into my essay on Certitude.'[15]

That last phrase reminds us that, at this period, Newman had at last succeeded in starting work on the *Grammar of Assent* and, in pointing us in that direction, suggests that where the relationships between the three 'offices' or 'functions' are concerned, there are epistemological as well as ecclesiological issues at stake.

Within the framework of the *Grammar*, it is in the dialectical relationship between 'religion' and 'theology', as a specification of the distinction between 'real' and 'notional' apprehension and assent,[16] that two of the three terms in the triad make their appearance. 'Religion', as 'real', is the expression of 'endurance', 'devotion', the 'priestly office', and 'theology', as 'notional', is the expression of 'thought', 'philosophy', the 'prophetical office'.

The relationship between 'religion' and 'theology' is dialectical: as the 1877 Preface will remind us, they mutually correct and enable each other. It would, nevertheless, be a mistake to conceive that relationship as symmetrical. It is, admittedly, true that, in the chapter on 'Apprehension and Assent in the Matter of Religion', Newman insists that 'Theology may stand as a substantive science, though it be without the life of religion; but religion cannot maintain its own ground at all without theology'.[17] But this is hardly to say more than that, as he had expressed it in his notebook a few years earlier: 'mere hereditary faith, in those who can have an intelligent faith is, to say the least, dangerous and inconsistent'.[18] If we were to appeal to a passage such as that just quoted from the

15 E. Sillem (ed.), *The Philosophical Notebook of John Henry Newman, Vol. II, The Text,* revised by A. J. Boekraad (Louvain, 1970), p. 167.
16 J. H. Newman, *An Essay in Aid of a Grammar of Assent* (London, 1870), pp. 55, 73. *(G.A.).*
17 *G.A.,* p. 121.
18 H. M. de Achaval and J. D. Holmes (eds), *The Theological Papers of John Henry Newman on Faith and Certainty* (Oxford, 1976), p. 86.

Grammar in support of any too straightforward or *simpliste* interpretation of the dictum that 'Theology is the fundamental and regulating principle of the whole Church system',[19] we should be doing violence to the unswerving thrust of Newman's lifelong polemic against rationalism in religion. Where the relationship between 'the way of reason and the way of practice'[20] is concerned, the depth of his commitment to the primacy of the practical, in man's quest for the knowledge of God, is so obvious and fundamental a theme in his writings as hardly to require illustration.

'"Knowledge of premises, and inferences upon them"', he said in that long extract from the *Tamworth Reading Room* which he cited in the *Grammar*, '"– this is not to *live*. It is very well as a matter of liberal curiosity and of philosophy to analyze our modes of thought; but let this come second"'.[21] Let this come second. Hence it is that 'no theology can start or thrive without the initiative and abiding presence of religion'.[22] Here is a claim which Newman endorses with his whole mind and heart, whereas when he admits that 'Theology may stand as a substantive science, though it be without the life of religion',[23] one senses that he is, as it were, warily holding the proposition at arm's length, with a pair of tweezers, fearful of contamination! One of the reasons, as I have briefly indicated elsewhere, why Newman, throughout his Catholic life, denied that he was a theologian, was that, although his conception of theological method underwent some modification between 1852 and 1878, it remained (and how could it not, in view of the state of Catholic theology at the time?) excessively intellectualist.[24] Times have changed, and with them conceptions of theology: the very grounds on which Newman denied that he was a 'theologian' may seem to us good reasons for ascribing the title

19 *V.M.I*, p. xlvii.
20 Newman, *Theological Papers*, p. 120.
21 *G.A.*, p. 95.
22 *G.A.*, p. 98
23 *G.A.*, p. 121.
24 Cf. N. L. A. Lash, 'Was Newman a Theologian?', *Heythrop Journal*, xvii (1976), pp. 322–5.

to him.[25] But this very fact should remind us, when interpreting passages in which he discusses 'theology' and 'theologians', that he was as suspicious of what he took to be 'theology' as he was of 'logic'. '"Logicians"', he said in that extract from the *Tamworth Reading Room*, '"are more set upon concluding rightly, than on right conclusions".'[26] Or, as he put it in his notebook in 1863: 'No ideas are more wild than those which are relentlessly reasoned out by the hard heart and the sober judgement.'[27]

The analogy between 'theology' and 'logic' provides a clue to the interpretation of that passage in the 1877 Preface with which we are principally concerned. 'Without external symbols to mark out and steady its course, the intellect runs wild', he writes in the *Grammar*, 'but with the aid of symbols, as in algebra, it advances with precision and effect.'[28] Excellently said: but we miss the irony at our peril. The passage continues: 'Let then our symbols be words: let all thought be arrested and embodied in words. Let language have a monopoly of thought; and thought go for only so much as it can show itself to be worth in language. Let every prompting of the intellect be ignored, every *momentum* of argument be disowned, which is unprovided with an adequate wording, as its ticket for sharing in the common search after truth. Let the authority of nature, commonsense, experience, genius, go for nothing. Ratiocination, thus restricted and put into grooves, is what I have called [formal] Inference, and the science, which is its *regulating principle*, is logic.'[29]

To ascribe to logic the status of the 'regulating principle' of

25 Yet even today Catholic theologians can hardly afford to ignore his warning, issued in 1884, that although 'Theology has its prerogatives and rights ... its very perfection as a science causes theologians to be somewhat wanting in tenderness to concrete humanity' (J. H. Newman, *On the Inspiration of Scripture,* edited by J. D. Holmes and R. Murray [London, 1967], p. 144).

26 *G.A.,* p. 94.

27 *Theological Papers,* p. 95.

28 *G.A.,* p. 263.

29 *G.A.,* p. 263, my stress.

human thought is to acknowledge its indispensability, and to indicate its function. Bremond was profoundly mistaken when he described Newman as a 'great despiser of reasoning'.[30] Nevertheless, a view of the 'authority' of logic such as that proposed in the *Grammar* should warn us against interpreting the ascription, to theology, of the status of 'regulating principle of the whole Church system',[31] in too exuberant a fashion. The theologian, at least as Newman conceived his function, is an indispensable technician.

I have been suggesting that the description offered, in the 1877 Preface, of the relationship between the 'priestly', 'prophetical' and 'regal' offices, should be read in the light of earlier versions of the triad. In particular, where the responsibility of the theologian to the living faith and worship of the community is concerned, I have suggested that the account offered of the relationship between 'devotion' and 'theology' should be read in the light of the analysis, in the *Grammar*, of the relationship between 'real' and 'notional' apprehension and assent. Except theology springs from, and reflects, the theologian's 'endurance', 'passion', 'devotion'; except it be the critical, theoretical reflection of the 'logic of the heart', it is corrupted by its own misconceived autonomy: it becomes the language of Balaam.

The thrust of my argument so far can be summarised by saying that the theologian, in reflecting on his responsibility to the faith of the community in which he stands, must remember that theology, as Newman conceives it, is a 'critical' and not a 'creative' power; that – to paraphrase the language in which the tenth *University Sermon* characterizes 'the distinct offices of Faith and Reason in religious matters' – theology may put its sanction upon the acts of religion without in consequence being the source from which religion springs.[32]

But, in that case, what are we to make of Newman's appar-

---

30 H. Bremond, *The Mystery of Newman* (London, 1907), p. 66.
31 *V.M.I*, p. xlvii.
32 Cf. J. H. Newman, *Fifteen Sermons Preached Before the University of Oxford* (London, 1871), pp. 183–4.

ent claim that theology 'has created both the Regal Office and the Sacerdotal ... [that] it has in a certain sense a power of jurisdiction over these offices, as being its own creations'?[33] I suggest that there is an ambiguity in this passage, an ambiguity stemming partly from Newman's practical concerns (he is, after all, writing a few years after the Vatican Council, with the ultramontane sea running high) and partly from his notion of 'revelation'.

The prophetical, priestly and royal offices constitute a 'triangle of forces' that is in principle, if I may so put it, an *equilateral* triangle. In practice, however, the triangle suffers distortion. In late nineteenth century Catholicism, there were plenty to speak up for the practical, 'religious' dimension of the Church's existence – for 'pastor and flock', and even more to speak up for the organisational, institutional dimension – for 'Pope and curia'. It was the relative autonomy of the *intellectual* dimension that was both practically and theoretically threatened: 'nor is religion ever in greater danger than when ... the Schools of theology have been broken up and ceased to be'.[34]

Therefore, although in the abstract any decision as to which of the three offices to take as starting-point for a sketch of the 'triangle' would be arbitrary, there were, in the concrete, excellent reasons for beginning with the Prophetical Office. Thus the laconic remark that the passage just quoted 'will serve as a proposition with which to begin',[35] expresses a practical, tactical concern. By beginning with the Prophetical Office Newman lays the emphasis, initially, where practical

33 *V.M.I*, p. xlvii.
34 *V.M.I*, p. xlvii. In June 1874, writing to Lord Blachford, Newman had said: 'I have long wished to write an Essay ... on the conflicting interests, and therefore difficulties of the Catholic Church, because she is at once, first a devotion, secondly a philosophy, thirdly a polity. Just now, as I suppose at many other times the devotional sentiment, and the political embarrass the philosophical instinct', C. S. Dessain (ed.), *Letters and Diaries of John Henry Newman, XXVII* (Oxford, 1975), p. 70.
35 *V.M.I*, p. xlvii.

rather than theoretical considerations demand that it be laid. That is the first point.

Secondly, we should notice that there is a syntactical ambiguity in the paragraph. 'Theology is the fundamental and regulating principle of the whole Church system. It [clearly 'theology'] is commensurate with Revelation, and Revelation is the initial and essential idea of Christianity.' But now notice, once again, the next sentence: 'It is the subject-matter, the formal cause, the expression of the Prophetical Office, and, as being such, has created both the Regal office and the Sacerdotal.'[36] Is the subject of that sentence 'revelation' or 'theology'? I suspect that the ambiguity is at least partly deliberate, a suspicion borne out by the fact that, in his first draft, Newman had said, not that theology was 'commensurate' with revelation, but that it was *synonymous* with it.[37]

And if this ambiguity admirably serves Newman's apologetic purpose, on behalf of the theological office, is it not, nevertheless, both dangerous and misleading? Does it not lead, only too easily, to just that idealist or rationalist misconception of the relationship between 'life' and 'language', 'living thought' and 'logic', 'religion' and 'theology', against which Newman waged relentless war from about 1830 to the end of his life? 'La révélation', says Professor Bergeron, 'exige d'être comprise rationellement; elle aspire à la théologie.'[38] Yes, but would it not be equally true to say that revelation contains an 'exigence' towards shared experience, 'endurance', 'devotion', 'religion', on the one hand, and towards social structure and organization on the other? At least the treatment, in 1840, of the unifying transformation, in Christ, of the 'three principal conditions of mankind',[39] would lead one to suppose so, as would the remark, in the third edition of the *Essay on Development,* that, 'one aspect of Revelation must not be allowed to exclude or to obscure another; and Christ-

36 *V.M.I*, p. xlvii.
37 Cf. Bergeron, p. 113.
38 Loc. cit.
39 *S.D.*, pp. 53–4.

ianity is dogmatical, devotional, practical all at once'.[40]

Newman's notion of the 'essential idea' of Christianity demanded a concept of revelation far wider and richer than any current in nineteenth century Catholic theology.[41] For want of such a concept, his treatment of revelation lacks consistency, inasmuch as he tended to work with a more 'propositional' notion of revelation than was compatible with his own best theological and philosophical insights. Thus, in the passage which we are considering, Newman, in bringing 'revelation' too unilaterally into close relationship with 'theology', implicitly appeals to an excessively intellectualist concept of revelation. I suggest, in other words, that the ambiguity to which I have referred is partly to be explained in terms of the tactical demands of controversy and partly in terms of weaknesses in Newman's theology of revelation. The 'regal' and 'sacerdotal' offices are, indeed, the 'creations' of revelation – the more or less effective transformations, by grace, of the 'conditions of mankind' – but they are not, or at least not in any straightforward sense, creations of *theology*.[42]

According to Professor Bergeron, if the action of the Church were only regulated by the principles specific to each of the three functions, then the unity of the Church would be seriously threatened. It is therefore necessary to discover 'regulating principles' capable of maintaining the balance of the whole. There are, according to his reading of the Preface, two such 'regulating principles': theology and the 'divine economy'.

As I see the situation, the unity of the Church is indeed permanently and seriously threatened by the divergent thrust of the three functions, each with its specific 'guiding principle' and 'instrument'. I further believe that, humanly speaking,

40 J. H. Newman, *An Essay on the Development of Christian Doctrine* (³London, 1878), p. 36. Newman began to prepare this edition in June 1877, as soon as he had finished revising the *Via Media*. For the corresponding passage in the first edition, cf. p. 35 of that (1845) edition.

41 Cf. N. L. A. Lash, *Newman on Development* (London, 1975), p. 98.

42 Speaking of 'worship', Newman says that 'Theology did not create it, but found it in our hearts, and used it' *V.M.I,* p. lxix.

the Church *has no resources* which it can deploy in order to maintain and recover its equilibrium. The tension, indeed frequently the conflict, between the three offices works itself out, *as* tension and conflict, both within the life, thought and experience of the individual Christian, whatever his office and ministry in the Church, and between the institutional elements of Christianity – without prospect or guarantee of harmonious resolution within the historical process. I say 'without prospect of resolution'. I do not say 'without hope'. The tensions, the conflicts, are experienced and undergone in hope, because they are the particular, practical expressions of faith in Christ, in whom alone the tensions are resolved, the functions harmonized. This hope is not unwarranted, this faith is not blind, because reflection on the life and history of the Church enables us to discern, with the eyes of faith, the power of God, the spirit of the risen Christ, 'regulating' the divine economy and maintaining in history the message of salvation.

If we would understand the complex, suggestive argument of the Preface we have to recognize that, beneath the description of theology as 'regulative' in a sense similar to that in which the function of 'logic' is thus described, there is another, more fundamental assertion of a quite different order at work. The 'divine economy' and 'theology', conceived as the human transcription of God's self-communicating presence and activity, are *theological* principles in two senses. They are theological in the sense that their recognition is an exercise of faith, of trust in the Spirit of God, and in the sense that they are the 'sacramental realisation' of the 'vector' of divine action in history. They are, in Newman's terminology, precisely *'principles'*, animating forces in a society,[43] not 'doctrines' – theoretical constructs that may be appealed to by parties in a dispute. Without their presence, which is the form of the presence of the Spirit of the risen Christ, the community of the Church would, indeed, blow apart or be definitively corrupted

43 Cf. Lash, *Newman on Development*, p. 108.

by the victory of either superstition, rationalism or *realpolitik*. Their presence enables the life of the Church, and of the individual Christian, permanently and necessarily characterized by conflict and tension, to achieve a measure of balance, of harmony, that is precarious, that is ever under threat from its own constitutive forces; it is a harmony whose assured achievement is eschatological.

Even these modest notes towards the reading of the 1877 Preface may, perhaps, have given some idea of what I take to be Newman's mature view of the relationship between the 'prophetical' and 'priestly' offices, and hence of his view of the relationship between the theological ministry and the life of the believing and worshipping community. I have said very little about the relationship between the 'prophetical' and 'regal' offices. A few words on this topic, by way of conclusion, will enable me to say something about the responsibility of the theologian to his conscience.

Christianity, in Newman's 'sacramental' vision of the Church, is, at one and the same time, life in the Spirit, language and organization. The 'priestly' and 'royal' dimensions of Christian existence are aspects of Christian 'praxis'. As such, they necessarily exist in tension with the quest for critical, reflective, theoretical expression of that praxis. For the theologian to discharge his responsibilities within the community, he must experience the tensions between the spontaneity of faith, the pragmatic exigencies of social order, and the critical quest of truth for its own sake, within his own life and experience. Only in the measure that he does so, can he hope appropriately to discharge his public office, an aspect of which is his responsibility to 'restrain' and 'correct' the 'extravagances' that are 'committed ... in the exercise of the regal and sacerdotal powers'.[44]

---

44 *V.M.I,* p. xlvii. The 'schola theologorum ... by the intellectual investigations and disputes which are its very life ... keeps the distinction clear between theological truth and theological opinion, and is the antagonist of dogmatism' *(Letters and Diaries, XXVII,* p. 338).

In so far as we consider the episcopate, including the papacy, as the institutional embodiment of the 'regal' office, there is no doubt, not only that theologians may find themselves in conflict with ecclesiastical authority, but that they should expect to do so. The 1877 Preface offers us, it seems to me, not only an outline of 'a theology of ecclesiastical abuses' but, more positively and less apologetically, a phenomenological sketch of those tensions and conflicts which are *constitutive* of the vitality and truthfulness of the Church.

According to John Coulson, with 'the introduction of theology as the regulating principle, Newman explicitly abandons his former distinction between life and form' (the distinction, that is, between 'prophetical' and 'episcopal' tradition),[45] 'by returning to Scripture for a threefold description of the Church as a community for teaching, worship, and ministry'.[46] That statement, I believe, demands qualification. It is undoubtedly the case that, in the 1877 Preface, Newman considers ecclesiastical authority only in its 'political' aspect, as the embodiment of the 'regal' function. But the earlier distinction had not been abandoned. It was central to Newman's view of papal infallibility, and of the distinction between the ministry of theologians and the teaching ministry of pope and bishops.[47] In other words, pope and bishops embody, in the terminology of the 1877 Preface, not only the 'regal' office but also (although this is not considered in any detail in the Preface)[48] an aspect of the 'prophetical' office. It is surely here, if anywhere, as a result of this structural differentiation within

45 For a sketch of the history of this distinction, cf. Lash, *Newman on Development*, pp. 122–34.

46 Coulson, pp. 172–3; cf. p. 170.

47 And it is this teaching ministry which is, in Newman's view, the ground and foundation of the Church's 'infallibility': 'the doctrine of the Church's infallibility is primarily an inference, grounded on the Church's office of *teaching*' (*Letters and Diaries, XXVII*, p. 79; cf. p. 84). Newman, as is well known, exhibits a certain distaste for the term 'infallibility': 'The most *real* expression of the doctrine is, not that [the pope] is infallible but that his decisions are "irreformabilia" and true' (*Letters and Diaries, XXVII*, p. 286).

48 It is referred to in passing: cf. *V.M.I*, p. lxxix.

the 'prophetical' or teaching office, that the theologian's
obligations to ecclesiastical authority might be expected to
conflict with his obligation to his conscience.

If, in the 1877 Preface, this problem is not considered in
detail, because of the particular formal aspect under which
ecclesiastical authority is presented, in the Letter to Norfolk
the problem is made to appear, in theory, patent of straightforward solution because of the sharpness of the distinction
which is drawn between judgements upon 'speculative truth'
and the practical character of conscience.[49] Thus it is that
Newman can insist that the authority of conscience (which, as
he reminds us, is at all times to be distinguished from its
contemporary 'counterfeit': namely, 'the right of self-will')[50] is
absolute. Conscience, because of its practical character, 'cannot come into direct collision with the Church's or the Pope's
infallibility; which is engaged on general propositions'.[51]
Therefore, since 'infallibility alone could block the exercise of
conscience, and the Pope is not infallible in that subject-
matter in which conscience is of supreme authority, no dead-
lock . . . can take place between conscience and Pope'.[52]

It all seems quite straightforward, and Newman is able to
combine the most vigorous defence of the inalienable rights of
conscience with unrestrained submission of all that he has
written, 'not only as regards its truth, but as to its prudence,
its suitableness, and its expedience', to the 'one Oracle of God,
the Holy Catholic Church and the Pope as her head'.[53] The
solution might not have seemed so straightforward had Newman adverted to the fact that his distinction between judgements upon 'speculative truth', and the practical character of
conscience, was oversharply drawn. After all, he had insisted,
in the Grammar, that conscience had not only a 'judicial' but

---

49 J. H. Newman, *Certain Difficulties Felt by Anglicans in Catholic Teaching, II*
     (London, 1876), p. 256. (*Diff. II*).
50 *Diff. II*, p. 250
51 *Diff. II*, p. 256.
52 *Diff. II*, p. 257.
53 *Diff. II*, pp. 346–7.

also a 'critical' office, and that it was not only a 'magisterial dictate', but also a 'judgement of the reason'.[54]

In 1876, Newman wrote to the convert, William Maskell: 'The Pope of the day may make himself one of his own partizans, and defend that view which is most favourable to himself – but since such comments are not *ex cathedra*, but the words of a private doctor, they do not impose an acceptance of the sense, which they advocate, on the consciences of the faithful.'[55] It is, however, absolutely clear that Newman believed that *'ex cathedra'* pronouncements *do* 'impose an acceptance on the consciences of the faithful', even if the duty of interpreting them, establishing their precise drift and significance, belongs to the *'schola theologorum'*.

Somewhere, there is a nettle that is not being grasped. Newman's failure to do so is, I believe, partly to be attributed to his temperament, and partly to a certain residual extrinsicism, or positivism, in his appreciation of the historically conditioned, contingent character of the magisterial acts of the 'episcopal' or 'apostolic' office.

It is also worth pointing out that, if by 'teaching' we mean the *declaration* of revealed truth, then the theological ministry is not, in Newman's view, strictly speaking a *teaching* ministry at all. It is interpretative, clarificatory, 'judicial' rather than 'legislative' or 'executive'; it is analogous to that ministry exercised by constitutional lawyers who, as he puts it, 'preserve the tradition of the British Constitution, in spite of King, Lords and Commons'.[56]

Even in our day, there are still those in high places – in curial offices and episcopal palaces – who operate with a more absolutist, less constitutionally diversified model of the Church. To such people, the recovery, on the part of

54 *G.A.*, p. 98.
55 *Letters and Diaries, XXVIII*, p. 25.
56 *Letters and Diaries, XXVII*, p. 212. It is to our purpose to notice that this analogy is offered as an illustration of the claim that 'the Schola Theologorum is (in the Divine Purpose, *I* should say) the regulating principle of the Church'.

theologians, of a sense of the relative autonomy, and irreducible specificity, of their ministry, is simply attributable to academic *hubris*. Similarly, where the Catholic faithful are concerned, it is still not easy, in certain quarters, 'to tell the party spirit, and the enthusiasm, and the sentiment unreasoning and untheological, of Catholics, that the Pope is *ever* to be disobeyed'.[57]

It must also, of course, be admitted that there are theologians who would reduce the function of papacy and episcopate to its 'political', administrative dimensions. If 'teaching' in the Church occurs in the exercise of *all three* 'offices', it would seem that there is an urgent need to differentiate between the 'doxological', 'declaratory' and 'critical' dimensions of the Christian quest for and expression of truth.

There are many reasons why it is hardly surprising that it is only now, a hundred years after it was written, that the 1877 Preface is really coming into its own. It still has much to teach us. We should, however, have radically misunderstood it if we sought to construct from it any theoretically satisfying systematic programme that would iron out conflicts and tensions, whether practical or theoretical, either within the experience of the individual theologian or in the relationships between the various dimensions and aspects of Christian existence.

If Church authorities are tempted prematurely to 'order' the life of the Church by the exercise of power, theologians are tempted to do so by the elaboration of theoretical solutions to practical problems. Both need to be reminded that 'whatever is great refuses to be reduced to human rule, and to be made consistent in its many aspects with itself'.[58]

Language and organization are at the service of life, and may not masquerade as its substitutes. And the life that they serve, and for which they seek forms of expression in 'thought' and 'active life' is confessed, in faith, to be the life of him whose achievement, as the historical transcription of the mystery of God, consisted in 'endurance'. He is, in his person and

57 *Letters and Diaries, XXVII*, p. 273.
58 *V.M.I*, p. xciv.

work, the incarnation of that truth which is 'to be received and transmitted, for he is our Prophet, maintained even unto suffering after his pattern, who is our Priest, and obeyed, for he is our King'.[59] But in him, and in following him, the dimensions of truth, both practical and theoretical, are not merely unified and coordinated, but are, in the manner of their unification, radically and paradoxically transformed.

59 *S.D.*, p. 62.

7. THE REMAKING OF DOCTRINE: WHICH WAY SHALL WE GO?[1]

There is, by now, widespread agreement concerning the inadequacy (and indeed, from many points of view, the positively misleading character) of the two most influential models of doctrinal 'development' that flourished between the mid-nineteenth and mid-twentieth centuries.[2] In his Hulsean lectures,[3] Professor Maurice Wiles proposes a third model, that of 'alteration of perspective'. In view of the frequency with which Wiles' theology is accused of being 'reductionist', it is worth noticing that, in offering this model, he declares his intention to be, in at least one significant sense, non-reductionist. Thus, using an example of which Newman was fond, he says: 'if one looks at a human face from a new angle, it may look very different, and yet one may at the same time be able confidently to identify it as the same face' (p. 7). It is clearly the *same* face that Wiles wishes to enable us to see, not some other face, or less of a face (one with the ears or the nose lopped off). And the context allows us to suppose that the face he hopes to enable us newly to see, in its wholeness, is the face of God in Christ.

Where the relation between 'contemporary doctrine' and its origins is concerned, he discusses (and too hastily disposes of

---

1 This essay is a slightly expanded version of one first published in the *Irish Theological Quarterly,* xliii (1976), pp. 37–43.
2 Cf. above, Ch. 4, p. 68. For a more detailed discussion, cf. N. L. A. Lash, *Change in Focus* (London, 1973).
3 M. F. Wiles, *The Remaking of Christian Doctrine* (London, 1974).

as unhelpful) what he calls the 'christological test'. Then he turns to what we might call the 'Spirit-test', and now a correct insistence on the freedom of the Spirit leads him to conclude that '*there cannot be any external tests* by which we can know if we are doing the job rightly or not' (p. 13, my stress). This seems to me too rapid. Surely he cannot mean, for example, that logical, historical, hermeneutical and ethical criteria (not all of which can be autonomously generated internally to the enterprise of *fides quaerens intellectum*) may not be invoked to help us to decide whether 'we are doing the job rightly or not'?

Christian sensitivity to the freedom of the Spirit, and hence to the unpredictability of the Spirit's activity in history, may encourage us to employ such criteria tentatively, carefully, interrogatively. But is this to say more than that the invocation of the doctrine of the freedom of the Spirit functions as the theological form of a warning that would be appropriate in any hermeneutical enterprise: namely, that the complexity and unpredictability of human, historical process renders inadvisable any knock-down, self-assured methodological dogmatism?

To say that 'external' criteria cannot furnish us with demonstrative, *a priori* proofs is surely correct, but to say that they cannot be used in *any* sense as 'tests' seems to me to overstate the case. Of course he is correct in saying that: 'We cannot provide in advance a *blueprint* of how doctrine is to be done' (p. 14, my stress), but the image of the 'blueprint' has subtly turned the notion of 'external criteria' into too easy an Aunt Sally.

Whether or not there may be 'external tests' available, Professor Wiles is going to need some basis, some method, on which to proceed. He therefore announces his two 'objectives', of 'coherence' and 'economy'. These objectives seem admirable ones for a doctrinal theologian, at least in the sense that a theologian whose declared objectives were 'incoherence' and 'unnecessary profusion' might be methodologically suspect.

But now things begin to get difficult. In describing the objective of 'economy', Wiles speaks of 'an insistence on distinguishing what the evidence *requires us to say* from what the evidence does not disallow us from saying' (p. 18, my stress). What kind of evidence could ever *require* us to say that 'God was in Christ, reconciling the world to himself'? Or, rather, what kind of requirement is here in question? It could hardly be merely historical. And if, as seems possible, it is some sort of logical requirement that he has in mind, then would this not exclude the possibility of any freedom for faith? (It might be interesting to pursue the suggestion that there would have to be a moral element in the notion of 'requirement', but this suggestion seems alien to the drift and tenor of the argument.)

Commenting on his decision to retain the concept of God, Professor Wiles remarks: 'When the principle of economy beckons me to dispense with the concept of God, I resist. To do so would be to leave a whole dimension of human experience even more opaque and inexplicable than it already is' (p. 108). In this sense, he believes that the evidence 'requires' him to retain the concept. 'It is not', he says, 'a matter of logical entailment; it is a matter of judgement of the kind that is essential to all historical and philosophical study. . . . What I am really challenging is the attitude that the traditional beliefs should always hold the field unless proved absolutely impossible (always of course a very difficult thing to do).'[4] His strategic concern is now clear but, for reasons hinted at in the previous paragraph, the notion of 'requirement' still strikes me as insufficiently precise, or specific, to be illuminating.

There is a further problem. What is the evidence concerning which we are, or are not, 'required' to say this, that or the other? And here it is not enough to ask: what is to count as evidence? Because if we answered (correctly), Scripture, tradition, our human and Christian experience, then we should soon discover that we had not made much headway towards the resolution of problems of theological norms and criteria. The more important question is: *How* does the evidence count? How is it to be marshalled? That is the question that I would like to unpack.

4 Personal communication.

I have already indicated, in the Introduction, why I have considerable misgivings concerning the terms in which debates about the 'starting-point' of theology in general, or of christology in particular, are currently cast. In particular, I am far from being convinced that it is either illuminating or coherent to speak of doing theology 'from above' or 'from below'.[5] However, if we agree to accept the terms of this debate, and if we assume that 'starting from above' means something like 'starting with God', and 'starting from below' means 'starting from our experience', then there is no doubt that Wiles wishes to be a 'from below' man. Far too summarily dismissing Karl Barth, whom he finds uncongenial, he says that 'we have no other starting-point [for our doctrine of God] than our ordinary human experience of the world' (p. 25). (*Whose* ordinary human experience? My discussion of Hans Küng, in the following chapter, will indicate why I find such formulations dangerously abstract.)

If I understand it correctly, the high scholastic, neo-aristotelean distinction between the two 'roads' along which 'scientific' activity proceeds is, to some extent, correlative to the contemporary distinction between proceeding 'from below' and 'from above' (not the least important point at which the analogy breaks down is that the medieval thinkers knew that it was necessary to journey in both directions, along both 'roads', whereas the contemporary debate supposes them to be alternatives). The medieval thinkers who employed this distinction took it for granted that enquiry started from where we are, from our experience, from how things seem to be. And our experience, simply *as* experience, is confused, bewildering, disordered. It puzzles, and raises questions. Accordingly, the first 'road', the '*via inventionis*', the way of discovery or enquiry, proceeded from how things seem to be, from an initially disordered mass of experience or data, from the *prius quoad nos*, to the heart of the matter, the 'essence', the *prius quoad se*. Then, having declared that X was the 'essence', the clue to under-

5 Cf. N. L. A. Lash, 'Up and Down in Christology', *New Studies in Theology, I*, ed. S. W. Sykes and J. D. Holmes (London, 1979).

standing, ordering and synthesizing that particular aspect of our experience which was under consideration, it was along the second 'road', the return journey, the *'via disciplinae'*, or way of confession and exposition, that, starting from the clue which was the term of the initial enquiry, the data in question were intelligibly ordered and patterned in the light of that clue.

Thus, for example, Christian theology along the *'via inventionis'* started from the experience of faith, of life, of suffering and death. It proceeded to reflect on that experience in the light of the words and work of Jesus of Nazareth: it thus raised questions about what he did and what was done in him; this raised further questions concerning who he was in whom these things were done; this, in turn, raised questions about who and how the God was in whom alone the earlier series of questions found intelligible resolution. Then, along the *'via disciplinae'*, the topics could be handled in reverse order: the doctrine of God, of the person of Christ, of the work of Christ and, finally, of the life of the Spirit (grace, church, sacraments). The same data were being handled along each movement of the *'duplex via'*, but the questions that arose would be different. Thus, for example, if, on the *'via inventionis'*, reflection on who it was in whom these things were done might raise the question: 'Are we then required (?) to say something like "this man is consubstantial with the Father"?', the correlative question on the *'via disciplinae'* might be: 'How is God this man?'.

My purpose in this essay is to suggest that it makes for incoherence to insist on working from 'below' while at the same time treating of the principal topics of a Christian theology in the order in which they arise along the *'via disciplinae'*. In attempting to indicate, as clearly as possible, some fundamental problems in theological method, I am, inevitably, oversimplifying matters. It is certainly no part of my argument that there is one and only one 'correct' ordering of topics or questions. Quite apart from anything else, the relationships between theological topics is rarely, if ever, 'linear'. Professor

Wiles regards the central chapters of his book as 'not so much a sequence as a series of contemporaneous investigations'.[6] Nevertheless, the chapters are in one sequence, rather than another, and part of my purpose is to suggest how and why it is that reflection on the doctrine of God (for example) that is in practice conducted (as Wiles conducts it in this book) more or less independently of christological, soteriological and ecclesiological considerations has a quite different 'feel' about it (and possibly reaches quite different conclusions) from reflection on the doctrine of God that arises from, is shaped and specified by, consideration of ecclesiological, soteriological and christological questions.

The order of Wiles' chapters is the order of the articles of the Creed. That is the clue which set me thinking, for this is the order of topics along the *'via disciplinae'*, along the way of confession and exposition, not along the *'via inventionis'*. Wiles tries to work 'from below' within each chapter, while retaining an overall structure that proceeds 'from above'. Let us see what happens, then, if we work *backwards* through the book, beginning with the chapter on grace and the spirit, in an effort to be faithful to Wiles' own recommendation that we should proceed 'from below'.

Chapter Five, on 'Grace and the Holy Spirit', begins: 'The central issue with which we are concerned in this whole study is the question: what ought one to believe about God and his relation to the world in the areas of central importance to Christian faith' (p. 83). Wiles mentions two difficulties which he has already discussed: problems of historical knowledge, and 'the difficulty inherent in ascribing universal effects to a particular historical occurrence' (ibid.). There then follow a series of what we may perhaps call 'Wilesian' moves: it is orginally the *strange* occurrence which is 'most readily grasped as evidence of God's spirit at work'; but eventually it is more 'ordinary' occurrences which 'come to be seen as the religiously most significant examples of that presence' (p. 85).

6 Personal communication.

One is familiar with such moves from much of Professor Wiles' work,[7] and they embody an extremely interesting and important insight. But a question seems to be being begged. If we grant that it is through experiencing the divine in the 'dramatic particular' that we most readily come eventually to perceive the divine at work in the 'humdrum', why should it not nevertheless still be the case that the 'dramaticality' of the particular has ontological and not merely pedagogical implications?

Discussing inspiration, he says that 'The traditional link between the Holy Spirit and the Bible should ... be understood as expressing the conviction that the biblical writings are of especial importance for man's grasping and responding to God's purpose for the world. It ought not to be understood to involve the need for any additional factor in the story of their emergence' (p. 90). But on what grounds is 'especial importance' ascribed to *these* writings for 'grasping' *God's* purpose for the world? Is this ascription of 'especial importance' solely a construction of man's religious sense, or is it a recognition, however unforced, of the status of the events to which the writings bear witness? If we have reason for saying that it is *God's* purpose that we discern in these events, does it not follow that, in some special sense, we ascribe the *events* to God? To put it more metaphysically: on what grounds is so sharp a distinction drawn between divine purpose and divine activity? (A thorough analysis of this chapter would, I believe, demand a questioning of Wiles' assumption that all talk of causality is talk of 'efficient causality', on the model of the action of material bodies one on another. It might be that, where discussion of causality in the context of grace and sacraments is concerned, we would do better to think in terms of what Karl Rahner calls 'quasi-formal causality'.)

Admittedly, such an ascription of events to God cannot be rapidly made. What I am suggesting is that if, more or less

7 Cf. e.g. M. F. Wiles, 'Does Christology Rest on a Mistake?', *Christ, Faith and History*, ed. S. W. Sykes and J. P. Clayton (Cambridge, 1972), pp. 3–12.

spontaneously, we ascribe 'especial importance' to the writings, then at least the question arises: is there an 'especial importance' to be ascribed to the events to which they bear witness? And that would be a question about what was going on in those events. Let us call it, in other words, a question about the 'work of Christ'. And so we are forced back to the topics discussed in Chapter Four, on 'The Work of Christ'.

This chapter begins with a discussion of four pictures of the work of redemption in Christ: the picture of victory over Satan, of 'satisfaction', of sacrifice, and of the reversal of the sin of Adam. The move here is a neat one. Wiles first translates these pictures into propositions that are quite compatible with almost any form of deism – thus the picture of 'victory over Satan' is interpreted to mean that 'evil ... [is unable] to destroy the personal being of man in God's world' (p. 65) – and then says, quite correctly, that this proposition does not demand the postulation of a particular act of God in history.

Wiles maintains that upholders of both 'objective' and 'subjective' theories of atonement will wish to say both that 'Christ's passion is in some way a demonstration of what is true of God's eternal nature' (p. 79), and that 'the passion of Christ has been remarkably effective in the transformation of human lives' (p. 80). That such transformation is significant, I agree. I would go further: were such transformation not to occur, the characteristic claims of Christian belief would have been falsified.

But I cannot accept that 'traditional objective language about the atonement' (p. 82) has been *simply* designed to express a combination of Wiles' two features of such language: 'eternal representation' and 'historical effectiveness' – in the narrow sense within which he restricts that latter notion. Before attempting briefly to articulate my disquiet, let me draw attention to the way in which the first of these two features which are common to all theories of atonement is described.

'Christ's passion is in some way a demonstration of what is true of God's eternal nature' (p. 79). How could we know that the passion demonstrates what is true of God's eternal nature if we did not have grounds for believing that, in that passion, God expressed his nature? And if that is correct, then are we not obliged to do what Wiles would have us systematically refrain from doing: namely, to speak of the Cross as an act of God? And not simply as any act of God, but as a special, historically particular act of God, because not even Professor Wiles, I think, would argue that in every historical event is God's eternal nature so insistently and, in one important sense, so unambiguously and luminously discerned to have been demonstrated.

As the argument of this chapter develops, I have the feeling that Wiles supposes that, if I may so put it, the full weight of a classical soteriology could be borne by Jesus simply considered as an individual, without reference to the rest of human history. Surely the early Christians, in their attempts to come to grips with the question: 'What was going on?' felt impelled to answer in terms of the whole historical and cosmic process? They felt, rightly or wrongly, that their coming to Easter faith entailed assertions to the effect that, in that one death, the whole course of history, including the future outcome of that history, was altered. This is admittedly a very curious conviction, and it impelled the further question: Who is this man, of whose death that sort of claim has to be made? In other words, questions arose concerning the person of Christ. So, back to Chapter Three, on 'The Person of Christ'.

The methodological inconsistency for the presence of which I am arguing begins to become strikingly apparent as Wiles mounts his critique of the concept of 'incarnation'. 'Written into the concept', he says, 'is the need to start from above; to begin with the being of God and then to consider his becoming man ... the whole thrust of the word "incarnation" seems to run counter to the lines of approach towards theological knowledge, which on general grounds we are most inclined to adopt' (p. 44).

He speaks of the need to be convinced that 'the evidence *requires'* incarnational belief (cf. p. 44). If my argument is sound, the evidence that could 'require' such belief would necessarily include that experience of faith, and that reflection on the 'work' of Christ, which originally gave rise to the appropriation of the concept of 'incarnation' (notice that I say 'appropriation of the concept', not: use of the metaphor) as a fitting category to express an answer to the question: Who is this whose 'work' is such that it has such consequence? But, given the order in which Wiles has chosen to treat of the various topics, he cannot include the 'work' as 'evidence' for the appropriateness of the concept of incarnation. Instead, he simply discusses problems of our historical knowledge of Jesus. Such problems are undoubtedly central, and exceedingly difficult, but excessive concentration on them at this point in the argument too narrowly restricts the framework of the enquiry.

Wiles speaks of a 'move from concentration on the figure of Jesus alone to concern with the whole Christ-event' (p. 54). But is this an accurate description of how the apostles and others first came to Easter faith and then, reflecting on the implications of that faith, came to redescribe the Jesus they had known in the days of his flesh? The move which he describes may be that which characterizes the order and direction of this chapter in his study, but would it not be more correct, where the early Church is concerned, to speak of 'concern with the whole Christ-event' leading to continual reassessment of the figure of Jesus?

The central problem with which the book is concerned: namely, that of the intelligibility of the notion of special divine activity,[8] is handled in this chapter in a similar way to that in which we saw that it was handled in the subsequent chapter, in which Wiles spoke of the passion of Christ as 'demonstrating what is true of God's eternal nature'. Here he says that 'Talk of his pre-existence might probably . . . be understood, on the analogy of the pre-existence of the Torah, to indicate

8   This is a central concern in much of Professor Wiles' recent work: cf. e.g. 'Religious Authority and Divine Action', *Working Papers in Doctrine* (London, 1976), pp. 132–47.

the eternal divine purpose being achieved through him, rather than pre-existence of a fully personal kind' (p. 53).

I am not at all sure that I understand what is meant by 'pre-existence of a fully personal kind'. But that is not the point I wish to make. If, in speaking of Jesus as 'the eternal Son of God incarnate', we are saying (as Wiles contends) that, through him, 'the eternal divine purpose [was] being achieved', how could we know that this was the case if we did not have grounds for believing that, in him, *God was achieving* his eternal divine purpose? But, if that is the sort of claim which we feel impelled to make, then, in view of the 'special' nature of that achievement (for which I have already argued, in the context of Chapters Five and Four) may it not be the case that, in attempting to spell out the implications of such a claim, and in discovering that some of these implications are ineluctably ontological, we may find ourselves saying something very like what was being said when it was affirmed of Jesus Christ that he is 'of one substance with the Father'? And so we are driven back to Chapter Two, on 'God', to reflect on the characteristics of a Christian doctrine of God.

Although this chapter determines the method and direction of the whole enterprise, we do not need to spend too much time on it. I will simply make three points. In the first place, a theology which resolutely refused to speak of God at all, and which spoke *only* of his 'effects', might well be a candidate for classification as 'reductionist'. However, in spite of his hesitations on this matter, and in spite of having adopted a position which he himself classifies as being in some sense 'deistic', Wiles does not so refuse. It is true that he wonders whether theology should perhaps abandon its claim 'to speak about the transcendent God ... in the sense that it will speak only of the effects of God as experienced, and make no attempt to speak of God in himself' (p. 25), but he nevertheless decides that 'it is doubtful whether one can properly claim to know the effects of something and yet be able to say nothing whatever about the thing itself' (p. 29).

In the second place, having admitted that 'the idea of some

special relationship of God to particular events is not to be excluded in advance as logically absurd' (p. 37), he goes on to claim that positive affirmation of such special relationship cannot, in fact, be justified. This is the ground on which, while denying that his view is 'deistic ... in that it allows for a continuing relationship of God to the world as source of existence and giver of purpose to the whole', he admits that the view is 'deistic in so far as it refrains from claiming any effective causation on the part of God in relation to particular occurrences' (p. 38).

In the third place, if the perspective from which I have been commenting has anything to commend it, then the trouble with this chapter is that, although it claims to be raising questions 'from within the Christian tradition' (p. 32), it is in fact an exercise in philosophical theology.

Now, I have no prejudice (as far as I know) against philosophical theology. But I fail to see how general philosophical (epistemological or anthropological) reflection on problems of transcendence could ever be expected to generate a specifically Christian doctrine of God. The most that such philosophical reflection could do would be to test and explore the extent to which Christians, reflecting on the sources and grounds of their faith, and in so doing coming to speak of God in the ways that they do, might be said to be speaking coherently and intelligently.

Moreover, I fail to see how the sort of 'evidence' admissible in such general philosophical reflection could ever be such as to 'require' us to speak of God as actively expressing himself, in a unique manner, in Jesus and in the life and faith of the Church. At most, such reflection might not 'disallow' Christians from so speaking. And so I am hardly surprised by the conclusions at which, in this chapter, Wiles arrives.

What he seems to be doing, in treating of the doctrine of God in the way that he does *before* he treats of the doctrine of Christ and the Spirit, is to establish the limits of Christian theological discourse in advance of any detailed discussion of its principal subject-matters. In other words, is he not doing just what, in his introductory chapter, he told us it was not permissible to do: namely, applying an 'external' criterion?

Is the general pattern or character of Wiles' account of Christian theology 'reductionist'? In intention, I have suggested, the answer is 'No'. He wants to enable us newly to see the whole face of God in Christ. In execution, at one level the answer is again 'No', in that he has deliberately refrained from eliminating or, as he puts it, 'dispensing with' the concept of God.

At another level, however, the answer seems to be 'Yes'. I have been suggesting that, at the heart of the sustained attempt to eliminate the necessity of 'belief in a specific incarnation in the person of Jesus' (p. 113), on the grounds that such a belief is not 'required' by the evidence, there are a set of methodological options that not only seem to be somewhat lacking in internal consistency, but which also violate his own stipulation that 'there cannot be any external tests by which we can know if we are doing the job rightly or not'.

8. REFLECTIONS 'ON BEING A CHRISTIAN'[1]

Pope Pius X, when Cardinal Patriarch of Venice, is said to have remarked of Loisy's *The Gospel and the Church*, 'Well, at least it's a theological work which isn't boring'. It cannot be said of every major theologian, as it undoubtedly can of Hans Küng, that he has never yet written a boring book. For that, if for little else, the inheritors of the mantle of Pius X should perhaps be grateful.

It is, indeed, remarkable that a theological work of over seven hundred pages,[2] one hundred of which are devoted to notes and bibliographical material, should have provoked such intense interest, both from Küng's fellow-theologians and from the general public. Küng insists that the book is '*only* an introduction' and 'merely *one* introduction' to 'Christian existence, action, conduct' (p. 20). Its 'aim' is 'to discover what is permanent' in Christianity, to establish what the Christian programme '*orginally* meant, before it was covered with the dust and debris of two thousand years' (p. 20). To that uncompromisingly negative assessment of Christian history, and the indications which it offers of Küng's methodological presuppositions, we shall return. I would like to begin, however, by acknowledging what seem to me to be the book's principal strengths.

In the first place, it is written with attractive and enviable clarity. Küng believes that, 'at a time of theological confusion and conceptual obscurity plain speaking is necessary' (p. 122).

1 First published in the *Month*, ccxxxviii (1977), pp. 88–92.
2 H. Küng, *On Being a Christian* (London, 1977).

Of course, the concept of 'plain speaking' is itself ambiguous. It may indicate a refusal to avoid the awkward question, to evade the humiliating admission. There is no doubt that Küng has the courage to call a spade a spade. If the Emperor has no clothes, he will say so; his preferred style of diplomacy is full-frontal. However, the concept of 'plain speaking' may also be used to suggest that whatever is worth saying can be said, and can be said simply. This is more questionable.

In the second place, this is an outstanding work of 'apologetics'. In modern times, 'apologetics' has often been a weapon of war, fashioned by a beleaguered Christianity out of materials singularly ill-adapted to the character and concerns of the Gospel. In Küng's hands, it is a persuasive, articulate, provocative *apologia* for Christian belief. It does not seek to bludgeon the reader by 'proof', but to persuade him towards taking the risk of seeing, and so sharing, that 'programme', as he calls it, which shapes and informs Hans Küng's own human and Christian hope.

In the third place, Küng is properly insistent, as was an earlier German-speaking spokesman 'on religion to its cultured despisers', on the interdependence of Christian speech and action, life and reflection.

In the fourth place, Küng's 'programme' is the following of Christ. The work is resolutely christocentric. Not only does Christianity exist 'only where the memory of Jesus Christ is activated in theory and practice' (p. 126), but 'everything can be called Christian which in theory and practice has an explicit, positive reference to Jesus Christ' (p. 125). The book begins with the question: 'Why should one be a Christian?' (p. 25) and it ends by answering: 'In order to be truly human' (p. 601), and by amplifying that answer in the form of a confession of faith: 'By following Jesus Christ man in the world of today can truly humanly live, act, suffer and die: in happiness and unhappiness, life and death, sustained by God and helpful to man' (p. 602). In common with many other readers, I am grateful for so honest, attractive and wide-ranging an *apologia* for the 'following of Christ'. Nevertheless, there are some questions that need to be raised.

Küng is committed, 'Right along the line', to 'an unbiassed *open-mindedness* for what is modern, extra-Christian, non-Christian, human, and for relentless criticism of our own positions, for dissociation from all ecclesiastical traditionalism, from dogmatism and biblicism' (pp. 36–7). And this commitment has as its object the rendering 'more precise, more relevant, more decisive' the 'meaning of the Christian reality' (p. 37). This sounds an admirably 'liberal' programme. The accents, however, are those of the Enlightenment and, remembering Gadamer's warning that 'the fundamental prejudice of the Enlightenment' was 'the prejudice against prejudice itself',[3] we are put on our guard. For instance, what notions of 'objectivity', of the relationship between meaning, expression and context, between truth and history, are presupposed in such a commitment to 'open-mindedness'?

Küng claims that, 'For the sake of faith in Christ and imitation of Christ we may and must speak today of Jesus more prosaically and less in the style of ancient festal inscriptions and festal forms of address, and also less in the style of Hellenistic professions of faith, but more in the style of the Synoptic Gospels and of present-day speech' (p. 450). That passage raises two distinct sets of questions. On the one hand, it raises questions concerning the relationship between the language of 'religion', of proclamation and preaching, and the language of 'theology', of critical reflection upon religious *praxis*. On the other hand, it raises questions concerning the pluralism of patterns of experience and action, and the corresponding pluralism of modes of 'present-day speech'. An illustration may help: Küng asserts that 'the ardently progressive technocrat' and the 'revolutionary Marxist' may both be Christians, provided only that it is Christian faith, and not 'scientific teleology', in the one case, and not 'Marx', in the other, that is 'ultimately decisive' (pp. 50–1). As a warning against false gods, against the identification of 'the Christian message' with

3 H.–G. Gadamer, *Truth and Method* (London, 1975), pp. 239–40.

'any existing or future social order' (p. 564), such a proviso is in place. But is it likely, or even possible, that the Christian technocrat and the Christian revolutionary Marxist either could or would articulate their Christian hope in a *common* conceptual and linguistic register the style of which could plausibly be characterized as that of 'the Synoptic Gospels and of present-day speech'? When I reflect on the fact that both Ian Smith and Robert Mugabe are, so far as I know, committed Christians, I find intolerably abstract recommendations to 'speak of Jesus' in the style of 'present-day speech' that seem to be untroubled by the complex urgency of the question: *whose* present-day speech?

It may seem odd to charge with abstraction a theologian who is so relentlessly hostile to theoretical discourse. Abstraction, however, takes many different forms. There is an abstraction which insensitively ignores the particular, the urgent, the personal (and of such abstraction, in theological work, both Hans Küng and I are suspicious); there is an abstraction which consists of attending to one thing at a time, which abstracts to select, not to ignore (and, in theological work, this is a manner of abstraction favoured by Aquinas and misunderstood by Küng, who tends to identify it with the first type); and there is an abstraction which consists in making unimpeachable general assertions, while insufficiently attending to the problem of their instantiation. Of abstraction, in this third sense, I find Küng guilty, again and again. Two examples must suffice.

'Just because the believer knows that his God is ahead, he can commit himself actively and at the same time in all his activity and commitment he can display an astonishingly superior indifference: unconcerned – like the birds of the air and the lilies of the field – trusting to God's providence and looking to the joyous future, he does not worry about food or clothing or at all about the next day' (p. 270). If I were, in a city in the third world, the unemployed father of several starving children, and a friend – similarly placed – sought, sharing my suffering, to enable me to share his hope by reflecting

together on the Sermon on the Mount, then it is indeed possible that he might thereby succeed in speaking to me of Jesus
in the style of the Synoptic Gospels and of present-day speech.
But if I, that same father, were to open Küng's book and read
that passage, it might well – as I heard him speak from his
social context to me in mine – engender, not hope, but cynic-
ism and anger.

A second example. 'The Church and its representatives
may, should and must take a stand publicly even on controversial social questions ... *wherever* and *as far as* the Gospel
of Jesus Christ itself (and not just any sort of theory) unambiguously (and not only obscurely) demands this' (p. 568). Is
the New Testament such, and is our historical relationship to
the New Testament such, that there are a significant number
of contexts in which such an unambiguous demand is unambiguously to be discerned? Is there not, in Küng's manner of
issuing his 'regulation', a failure of attention to those irreducibly complex mediations, of life and thought, of practice and
interpretation, sustained attention to which is a necessary
condition of critically grounding claims to discern, in specific
situations, the command of God in Jesus Christ? And may it
not perhaps be the case that attention to the conditions under
which such mediations might effectively be perceived and
negotiated has been one of the characteristic concerns of that
bimillenial Christian effort of interpretation and redescription
to which Küng sits so lightly? In other words, does not his
confidence in the possibility of straightforwardly carrying out
his programme to speak of Jesus in the style of today's speech
suggest that he is insufficiently attentive to problems of hermeneutics?

Küng is rightly concerned that the Jesus of whom we speak
should be the 'real Jesus', and not a product of our desires,
hopes or ideological preferences. 'The question of the truth
now becomes so much more urgent: which Christ is the true
Christ? ... The *dreamed-up* or the *real Christ*?' (p. 145). Put like
that, few of us would opt for the 'dreamed-up' Christ. But
what concept of 'reality' is presupposed in that manner of

making the distinction between truth and falsehood? This question is not easy to answer. At times, a distinction is drawn between 'poetry' and 'reality' (p. 127; cf. pp. 139–40). At times, however, we are reminded that 'poetry occasionally comes closer to the mystery of nature and of man than the most accurate description or photograph' (p. 415). At times, the question (raised in the context of Jesus' miracles) 'What really happened?' invites and receives a conjectural answer that seems to presuppose a somewhat questionable concept of historical facticity: 'Can [the historian] get at the reality *concealed behind* the popular narratives?' (p. 229, my stress). At times, however, we are reminded that 'truth is not the same as facticity and in particular not equivalent to historical truth. As there are *different forms and strata of reality*, so there are different forms of *truth*' (p. 415).

I would wish wholeheartedly to endorse Küng's conviction that, where the truth or falsehood of the confession of Christian faith is concerned, certain questions of historical facticity are of central and irreducible significance. And yet, underlying the unclarity, perhaps inconsistency, that attends his uses of the concept of the 'real', I believe that I can detect that which Bernard Lonergan regards as the father and mother of all epistemological confusions: namely, the assumption that knowing consists in 'taking a look'. Thus, the 'real' is too easily presumed to be the 'observable' (even if the concept of 'observation' is sometimes confessedly metaphorical), rather than that which is affirmed in true judgements.

Such an assumption would, at any rate, be of a piece with Küng's apparent conviction that the 'real Jesus' can, as it were, be 'read off the page' of the New Testament, by any reasonably 'open-minded' critical historian. Even if we allow for the tendency, in recent years, to swing away from an unqualified scepticism where the possible outcome of quests of the 'historical Jesus' is concerned, Küng seems over sanguine in regard to the number of things that can confidently be asserted concerning the character, sayings and intentions of the pre-Easter Jesus.

It is especially where our knowledge of the pre-Easter Jesus is concerned that, in placing the weight that he does on scientific-historical recovery of the essence of Christianity, Küng stands unfashionably close to a strategy reminiscent of late nineteenth-century Liberal Protestantism. On the other hand, in the matter of style, of bewitching (if repetitive) rhetorical tone, I was more conscious than in the case of several of his previous books of his abiding debt to Karl Barth, for whom so heavy an emphasis on the pre-Easter Jesus, thus recovered, would have been unwelcome. Perhaps we might say that the voice is the voice of Karl Barth, but the hands are the hands of Harnack!

Moreover, because Küng seems not to find it necessary to obey Gadamer's prescription (against Dilthey and Bultmann) to respect 'the strangeness of the text',[4] he can not only 'read off' a great deal with surprising assurance, but can 'apply' the meaning discerned in the text with comparable facility. Thus, he at one point describes the aim of the book in terms of translating 'the titles and ideas of former times into the outlook and language of our own' (p. 389; it is a pity that he is not familiar with Professor David Kelsey's illuminating criticism of the metaphor of 'translation').[5] But how is this project to be executed? Is it, for example, as straightforwardly certain as Küng seems to think that 'Che Guevara ... or Camillo Torres have less right than Gandhi or Martin Luther King to claim Jesus as their example' (p. 189), or that '*Non-violence* can always find support in *Jesus Christ,* the *use of violence* perhaps in an emergency can find support in reason' (p. 570)?

Küng is, of course, well aware of the fact that hermeneutical problems exist. 'Even the theologian must not speak in a merely abstract way about social relativity' (p. 211). He therefore seeks 'to see Jesus of Nazareth as he really was, in his

4 The phrase is Geoffrey Turner's, in 'Wolfhart Pannenberg and the Hermeneutical Problem', *Irish Theological Quarterly*, xxxix (1972), p. 115; cf W. Pannenberg, 'Hermeneutic and Universal History', *Basic Questions in Theology, Vol. I* (London, 1970), p. 118; Gadamer, *Truth and Method*, pp. 273–4, 295–9.

5 Cf. D. Kelsey, *The Uses of Scripture in Recent Theology* (London, 1975).

social context'. Only then can Jesus 'become significant –
despite his strangeness – today even in our social context'.
Such a method of interpretation 'allows for both *historical distance in time* and *historical relevance at all times*', enabling us 'to
discover important constants despite all variables' (ibid.).

What are the 'constants', and how are we to handle the
problem of their discernment and application? For Küng, the
uniqueness of Jesus is to be found in the fact that he transcended and thus refused to be identified with any one of the
'corners' of a 'quadrilateral' of styles of human *praxis*: 'Establishment, revolution, emigration, compromise' (p. 211).

'Jesus did not belong to the ecclesiastical and social establishment' (p. 177); he was 'neither a supporter of the system
nor a politico-social revolutionary' (p. 187); 'neither did he
want to opt out of ordinary life, to be an ascetic monk' (p.
200); fourthly, 'Jesus was not a pious legal moralist' (p. 207),
seeking a life of 'realistic', practical compromise. He 'seems to
have something of the most diverse types . . . but for that very
reason does not belong to any one of them' (p. 212). The
reason 'why he cannot be classified either with the ruling
classes or with the political rebels, either with the moralisers
or with those who have opted for silence and solitude' (p. 262)
is that his radicalism is 'the radicalism of *love*', not 'the radicalism of an ideology' (ibid.). And the titles attributed to him in
the New Testament 'are tacit or even explicit *challenges* to all
. . . who *themselves want to set the ultimate standards*' (p. 388).

The Christian who seeks to follow Christ must actualize, in
the pattern of his commitment, the same freedom in respect of
the 'quadrilateral'. But then, which way will he move? 'If
someone does not want to tie himself to the establishment, or
. . . to support the cause of revolution, if he will not decide for
local or mental emigration and yet rejects moral compromise,
what does he really want? . . . What is the supreme norm?' (p.
238). The answer is clear: 'The supreme norm *is the will of God*'
(p. 242).

But, if there is an important sense in which obedience to the
will of God relativises particular commitments, being obedi-

ence to the mystery that transcends all particular human programmes and visions; if Küng rightly wishes to stress that, for the Christian, the only ultimate absolute is the absolute mystery of God, is there not nevertheless something unsatisfactory about the way in which he 'applies' his account of Jesus' commitment, and of Jesus' freedom, to the options available to the individual Christian and to the Christian community? I have already indicated the manner in which the pattern is applied to the individual; its ecclesiological application runs as follows: 'the Church is faced with the same religio-social basic positions and basic options, involved in *the same quadrilateral choice* between establishment, revolution, retreat and compromise, in which Jesus was involved ... the christological indicatives become the ecclesiological imperatives' (p. 504).

What Küng is doing is taking a short cut past those practical and theoretical historical mediations of meaning which create that 'distance' between Jesus and ourselves which hermeneutics seeks to overcome. I am not saying that this 'distance' *cannot* be overcome, but that it can only be overcome in particular times and places, by particular forms of speech and action. If we attempt, this side of the reign of God, to overcome the distance in completely *general* patterns of action and speech we evade, by illegitimate abstraction, the particularity (and agony) of concrete choice and affirmation. Thus, for example, Küng says that 'it is possible to follow [Jesus] without an explicitly political or socio-critical commitment' (p. 187). Yes, but is it possible so to follow him in *all* situations, in *every* time and place? Or again: 'We must therefore again insist ... that a *Christian can be a socialist* (against the "right"), but a *Christian is not bound to be a socialist* (against the "left")' (p. 567). But are there not particular situations in which obedience to the 'supreme norm' may indeed, in the concrete, take the form of an *obligation* to be, or not to be, a 'socialist'?

The fundamental weakness (as I see it) which I am trying to bring into focus may become clearer if we contrast Küng's approach with that of Karl Barth. Barth's insistence that 'properly speaking, there is no such thing as dogmatic tolerance',[6] was not simply an expression of narrow confessional-ism. He knew that 'the real Christian faith can be recognised, lived and expressed only in the relativity and determinateness of a specific place'.[7] He trusted, in faith, that, in the interaction (sometimes conflictual, sometimes cooperative) of a multiplicity of patterns of behaviour and discourse, the Word of God would find obedient witness and expression. But he refused the illusion of the man who, seeking to stand *outside* all 'specific places', attempts an olympian neutrality or 'pan-contextuality' of action or speech. To this illusion Küng has, I believe, unintentionally succumbed.

If my unease concerning the manner in which problems of hermeneutic are handled in this book is at all justified, and if I am right in thinking that Küng's interpretative strategy is partly attributable to the influence of certain epistemological presuppositions, then we would expect to find theoretical, formal patterns of discourse and reflection regarded with grave suspicion. And, sure enough, we do. 'The Christian concept of truth', we are told, 'is not – like the Greek – contemplative-theoretical, but operative-practical' (p. 410). But is there any such thing as *'the'* Christian concept of truth? Can we really not do better today than simply repeat crude and clichéd contrasts (as philosophically jejune as they are historically indiscriminate) between 'Hebrew' and 'Hellene', 'Athens' and 'Jerusalem'? Is it not possible resolutely to opt, as Newman did, for the primacy of the practical, the concrete, the personal, and yet to acknowledge (as Newman also did) the indispensability, in its place and for its purpose, of more sheerly theoretical, formal aspects of the quest for understanding? For my part, I confess that when I find centuries of Christian reflection on the mystery of God dismissed as 'increasingly pretentious, intellectual speculation on the Trinity', amounting to no more than a kind of 'higher Trinitarian mathematics' (p. 472), I begin to suspect that we are faced

6   K. Barth. *Church Dogmatics, I/2* (London, 1956), p. 823.
7   Op. cit., p. 824.

with an only too familiar lack both of historical imagination and conceptual rigour.

Is there, or is there not, an irreducible variety of forms and levels of discourse, for no single one of which it may be claimed that it, and it alone, is an appropriate vehicle for Christian speech and enquiry? Küng's answer is to the effect that 'It has now become very much clearer that the *God of the philosophers* and the *God of Israel and of Jesus* cannot be brought into a superficial harmony . . . the relationship must in fact be seen in a genuinely dialectical way: the "God of the philosophers" is – in the best Hegelian sense of the term – "cancelled-and-preserved" (*aufgehoben*) positively, negatively and supereminently in the "God of Israel and of Jesus" ' (p. 309). To accept the historical implications of that assertion is to agree with Küng (and Harnack) that the greater part of the history of Christian systematics has consisted in a lamentable regression to pre-Christian concepts of God. But perhaps the question should concern not the multiplicity or unity of gods, but the multiplicity or unity of forms and levels of discourse concerning God. And perhaps the history of Christian theology may be seen as the story of recurrent, now more, now less successful attempts to achieve and sustain appropriate differentiations of patterns of discourse, and appropriate modes of interaction between them.

The problem of discerning the 'constants' amidst the 'variables', of specifying – if you like – the 'essence of Christianity', is both urgent and perennial. My contention has been that the strategy which Küng adopts unwittingly abstracts from the variety of contexts in which, concretely, Christians speak and act, and that his suspicion of the theoretical has led him to misconceive the nature of the hermeneutical task. The point is, of course, that these weaknesses are two sides of the same coin. If we would seek, not merely appropriately to speak and act in specific situations, but also (as theologians) reflectively to think through and critically ground the forms of such speech and action, then there is no available short cut past the almost impenetrable thickets constituted by the practical and theoretical mediations of meaning and truth in history. Paradoxically (and here again I have, at the back of my mind, Newman's distinction between 'notional' and 'real' assent) it may be that the inquisitive, tentative character of good theoretical reflection is, in the long run, a more fruitful partner of the commitment of faith than is a mode of theological discourse which mistakenly assumes that there is, or should be, some one single form of 'present-day speech', and that a form which is straightforward, 'plain' and universally available.

On Being a Christian was received, in many quarters, with considerable enthusiasm. This enthusiasm I partly share: I have already said that, as apologetic, it is a considerable achievement. If, however, I have concentrated, not on its general impact, or on Küng's handling of this or that New Testament passage, or of this or that particular doctrine or aspect of Christian practice, but on apparently more obscure and recondite matters, I have done so because, by more or less identifying the apologetic and theological tasks, Küng may have given the impression that there are, after all, impartial and comparatively straightforward programmatic solutions to contemporary problems of Christian belief and action. I have tried to indicate some of the reasons why I do not believe this to be the case. If we wish to avoid both mystification and disillusionment, we would do well to bear in mind Fergus Kerr's warning that 'an enormous amount of hard work is all that faces the student of theology at the present time'.[8]

8 F. Kerr, 'Beyond Lonergan's Method', *New Blackfriars*, lvii (1976), p. 71.

PART FOUR:
ASPECTS OF BELIEF

Even if questions of theological method are, in some respects,
more fundamental than questions of content, the distinction
between 'method' and 'content' cannot be too tightly drawn
without distorting the character and concerns of Christian
theological enquiry. Even if one insists, for example, as I did
in Chapter One, that it is a mistake to suppose that the languages of 'religion' and 'theology' should – considered as types
of discourse – necessarily be 'similar', this defence of theology's right to its own technicality of method and expression
must not be taken as entitling the theologian to claim immunity from the question: But what does it *mean*? And if Christians
are sometimes adept at failing to *locate* their beliefs in the
context of other aspects of their human speech and behaviour,
of failing to make *connections* between the language of belief and
the other languages by means of which they order their
experience, then it falls to the theologian to seek the location,
to press the connections. Accordingly, in these last three
essays, I have sought to 'put the method to work' in respect of
certain aspects of the doctrines of salvation (Chapter Nine),
divine providence (Chapter Ten) and eternal life (Chapter
Eleven). If the results appear to be confusing and even, to
some people, disturbing, this is perhaps partly because, to the
extent that we insulate the language of belief from the secular
languages that we employ, we invest it with a spurious and
illusory clarity.

9. THE CHURCH AND CHRIST'S FREEDOM[1]

'If you continue in my word, you are truly my disciples, and you will know the truth, and the truth will make you free.'[2] According to that promise, truth is discovered by dwelling in Christ's word; and the truth that is thus discovered is a truth that liberates. The Church is the community of those who seek to 'hear the word of God and do it'.[3] We could perhaps go on from here and assert that the Church, the community of Christian belief, expresses, embodies and proclaims man's freedom in God.

But would such an assertion be true? Many people would unhesitatingly answer: 'No'. They would say that the Church is too deeply enmeshed in a web, woven by history, which has irredeemably entwined its structures and attitudes with just those economic, social and political forces which, at least on a world scale, stifle or inhibit man's search for freedom. Moreover, if men are to be freed, they must be enabled critically to confront, and come to grips with, the roots of their alienation; whereas Christian preaching and worship are ideological expressions of man's alienated condition and, as such, they distract men from the task of liberation. In other words, the Church, in its structures and in its consciousness, masks rather than expresses, frustrates rather than embodies, denies rather than proclaims, the freedom of man, the freedom of the sons of God.

1 First published in *Concilium*, Vol. 3, no. 10 (1974), pp. 98–109.
2 John viii, 31–2.
3 Luke viii, 21.

Others would, equally unhesitatingly, answer: 'Yes'. The freedom of which the gospel speaks is interior, religious, eschatological. And of *this* freedom the Church, the community of Christian belief, continues to be both an expression and an embodiment. Salvation is found in the Church.

It is tempting to generalise, and to suggest that one of the most fundamental lines of division separating Christians today is that drawn between the two types of answer I have sketched. But it is impossible to know whether the original assertion is true or false, and in what sense and within what limits, unless we know what that assertion means. My initial concern, therefore, is the modest one of trying to throw some light on what it might mean to assert that the Church expresses, embodies and proclaims man's freedom in God.

Freedom and Salvation

What do we mean by 'man's freedom'? John Robinson has remarked that, if you try to 'net' the concept of freedom 'in the categories of discursive knowledge, let alone capture it in a verbal definition . . . it slips through your fingers, and you end up, as deterministic philosophies do, by concluding that it does not exist'.[4] Let me, therefore, shift the emphasis: what do *we* mean by 'man's freedom'? We (assuming, for the moment, a Christian readership for these essays) are Christian men and women. Therefore, in asking questions about freedom, we are asking questions about *human* freedom, because we are men and women. We are asking questions about *Christian* freedom, because we are men and women who seek to interpret their existence in the light of the mystery of Christ.

Are these *two* freedoms? And, if so, how are they related one to another? Or are they two names for one single freedom? And, if so, what distinctive contribution might we be expected to make, as Christians, to the expression and embodiment of this one freedom of man? Such questions are, of course, ulti-

4 J. A. T. Robinson, *Christian Freedom in a Permissive Society* (London, 1970), p. ix.

mately christological, as their form indicates. (Indeed, for some theologians, the concept of freedom is the defining centre of their christology.)[5]

When, in our search for the meaning of Christian freedom, we turn to the Scriptures, we find ourselves caught up in a cluster of methodological problems. Thus, for example, if we were to assume that there is a more or less one-to-one correspondence between our contemporary concepts and their nearest terminological equivalents in the Scriptures (an odd assumption, but one not uncommonly made), then we would investigate the connotations of the concept of 'freedom' in the Old and New Testaments. We should find that the words 'free' and 'freedom' are almost always used, in the New Testament, only in a theological sense which is not, as such, directly based upon the Old Testament, but which seems rather to reflect Greek usage in the secular culture in which the New Testament was born.

Amongst the biblical concepts or families of concepts whose range of meaning closely corresponds to modern concepts of 'freedom' and 'liberation', that of 'salvation' is of particular interest. The Hebrew root whose derivatives are usually translated by 'salvation' and cognate terms seem primarily to refer to 'the possession of [living] space and the freedom and security which is gained by the removal of constriction'.[6] Hence, in the pre-exilic period, the concept of salvation is that of military victory, and of rescue and liberation from *any* trouble – from foreign domination, from poverty, from illness. After the exile, an increasing emphasis on the future, and a deepening messianic hope, gave a new note of ultimacy to the concept. It now acquired overtones of total, unshakeable, everlasting victory and liberation for God's people. Thus the concept of salvation 'approaches the idea of liberation from all evil, collective and personal, and the acquisition of complete security'[7] and peace.

5 Cf. P. Van Buren, *The Secular Meaning of the Gospel* (London, 1963).
6 J. L. McKenzie, *Dictionary of the Bible* (London, 1966), p. 760.
7 McKenzie, op. cit., p. 761.

We are exploring the relationship between 'human freedom' and 'Christian freedom'. From our point of view, therefore, it is of fundamental importance to notice in what sense the Old Testament concept of salvation is a *theological* concept. It is a theological concept not in the sense that it refers to problems and experiences other than those of day-to-day human, historical existence, but in the sense that, for the Hebrew, all victory and liberation from evil, collective or individual, present or future, is ascribed to the activity of God, to the God who sets his people free.

In the New Testament, the same cluster of meanings are retained but now, under the influence of the Greek words chosen to express the biblical concepts, 'salvation' acquires new overtones of healing, wholeness, well-being, health. The frame of discourse within which the concept is employed is one in which considerable emphasis is placed on the ultimacy, the finality of the salvation wrought by God in Christ. There is also, in contrast to the Old Testament, a marked concentration on the individual, 'interior' aspects of salvation: salvation as 'seeing', for example, or as 'hearing'. But these are shifts of emphasis, surely, not a rejection of the broader frame of reference which characterized the Old Testament context. Even in its final New Testament usage, the concept of salvation still retains the resonances acquired during its long history. In other words, it is of fundamental importance to notice that the concept of salvation in the New Testament is a theological concept in the sense that liberation from all evil, collective or individual, present or future, is ascribed to the activity of God in Christ.

It could be objected that the point which these preliminary observations have been concerned to make might have been more succinctly expressed in Aquinas's phrase: '*Omnia autem tractantur in sacra doctrina sub ratione Dei.*'[8] This is true, but all of

---

8 'All things are dealt with in holy teaching in terms of God', *Summa Theologiae, Vol. I, Theology*, ed. T. Gilby (London, 1964), pp. 26-7. I believe that the context permits that emphasis on '*all* things' to which I appeal in the text.

us, Catholics and Protestants, are heirs of centuries of Christian schizophrenia which had encouraged us continually to lose sight of, or even explicitly to deny, the significance of that 'Omnia'. To put it as starkly as possible, whatever distinctions need to be drawn between our relationship to God and our relationship to the historical conditions of our human existence, we are not doubly enslaved and doubly freed. There is not economic, political, psychological slavery and also the slavery of sin. There is not economic, political, psychological freedom and also the freedom with which Christ has set us free. The slavery and freedom of which politicians, economists, sociologists and psychiatrists speak is the slavery and freedom of which Christian preaching and theology speak. To suppose otherwise is to fall victim to an anthropological dualism (between 'spirit' and 'matter', for example) which has little biblical and less contemporary warrant. Christian preaching and theology, however, have the specific responsibility of speaking of this human freedom, of each and every human freedom, *sub ratione Dei*. With this in mind, let us now return to the assertion with which we began.

The Church, the community of belief, expresses, embodies and proclaims man's freedom in God. Is this assertion true? It is true that the Church has never lost sight of the fact that its fundamental duty is to proclaim and to embody the liberation, the healing and salvation of man by God. But, if I am correct in suggesting that the concept of salvation, the Christian concept of freedom, is a theological concept in the sense that, to Christian faith, all liberation from all evil is ascribed to the action of God in Christ, then it is also true that the Church has frequently misunderstood this duty. It has frequently spoken and acted as if its responsibility were, not to speak of human freedom *sub ratione Dei*, but to speak of some other freedom only obscurely and tangentially related to that freedom for which we hope, for which we work, and which we partially and incipiently experience, as human beings. At best, the Church has frequently spoken and acted as if its only concern was with the interior, psychological or moral aspects of the freedom of the individual or as if its only duty, in the midst of human slavery, was to proclaim that, in the end, beyond the end of time, man will be fully free.

'Equality', said Hegel, 'was a principle with the early Christians; the slave was the brother of his owner. . . . This theory, to be sure, has been retained in all its comprehensiveness, but with the clever addition that it is in the eyes of Heaven that all men are equal. . . . For this reason, it receives no further notice in this earthly life.'[9] Something similar is the case in respect of the Christian proclamation of salvation. By means of the 'clever addition' we have been led to misconceive the sense in which salvation, liberation or freedom are 'theological concepts'. As a result, the extent to which the Church has, in practice, been concerned effectively to express, embody and proclaim the freedom of man has been dramatically restricted.

It does not follow that the rejection of our initial assertion as false (a rejection which I outlined at the beginning of this essay) can be endorsed without qualification. It would be historically absurd to deny the contribution which Christianity has made, and continues to make, to the liberation, the freeing, the healing and hoping, of man – both collectively and individually. Nevertheless, if we are really to meet the challenge with which the contemporary rejection of the community of the Church confronts us, we must face up to the implications of the fact that the critics of 'institutional Christianity' are, increasingly, men and women whose deepest human and Christian hope is that the Church might, convincingly and effectively, express, embody and proclaim man's freedom in God. The enemies of the gospel do not criticize the Church. They ignore it.

The Church and Man's Freedom
It is from Christ that the Church draws its life, its meaning and its power. The Church, in so far as it *is* the Church, lives

9 G. W. F. Hegel, *Early Theological Writings* (Philadelphia, 1971), pp. 88–9.

by the Spirit of the risen Christ. If we ask, therefore, how the Church might less inadequately discharge its responsibility to express, embody and proclaim man's freedom in God, we are asking about the relationship between Christian freedom, today, and the freedom of Christ. By reflecting on that relationship we can also cast some light on a question which was touched on earlier, namely: what distinctive contribution might we be expected to make, as Christians, to the freedom of man?

From the perspective within which this essay is written, the fundamental structure of the Church's relationship to Jesus may most conveniently be expressed in terms of *remembrance*.[10] We 'continue in his word' to the extent that we faithfully hear that word and do it. The freedom for which we work and hope will be that freedom which *he* expressed, embodied and proclaimed, only in the measure that we succeed in 'remembering' his freedom faithfully, without distortion or diminution.

At this point, the theologian is tempted to indulge in some purely formal, abstract discussion of the nature of such 'remembrance'. And this, in the twentieth century, he may not do. We cannot evade the implications of what Peter Berger has described as the 'root proposition' of the sociology of knowledge, a proposition derived from Marx: namely, that 'man's consciousness is determined by his social being'.[11] How are we to ensure that our remembering of Jesus, which will determine our understanding of the freedom for which we seek, is not an illusion; that it is consciousness, and not false consciousness? If we brush this problem aside, then our Christian self-understanding (and thus also our preaching and theo-

10 This statement should not be understood as if my intention were reductionist. There are other aspects of the Church's relationship to Jesus the examination of which would demand the use of other models. Thus, for example, I wholeheartedly endorse the insistence on the inescapable function of ontological considerations in christology expressed in D. M. MacKinnon, 'Substance in Christology – a Cross-Bench View', *Christ, Faith and History,* ed. S. W. Sykes and J. P. Clayton (Cambridge, 1972).
11 P. L. Berger and T. Luckmann, *The Social Construction of Reality* (London, 1971), p. 17.

logy) will be, in a pejorative sense, merely ideological.[12] As such, it will, in the long run, contribute not to the freedom of man but to the perpetuation of his enslavement.

In any society, existing social structures, beliefs and attitudes are strengthened and legitimated in so far as it can plausibly be maintained that things have ever been thus, and that the way things are is, fundamentally, the way that God wills them to be.[13] Thus, for example, when received notions of 'salvation' are challenged, the challenge is likely to be resisted on the grounds that the alternative account offered is 'untraditional' or 'unbiblical'. This may, indeed, turn out to be the case. But it is just as likely that the fundamental grounds of the resistance is the threat which the challenge poses to existing structures, practices, self-understanding and identity. Beneath the battle of words in theological debate there is often a deeper struggle engaged, of which the participants may well be unaware. Moreover, it is important not to lose sight of the fact that the process of legitimation is necessary for the social transmission of beliefs, attitudes and values. We may, indeed, be obliged critically to question our legitimations but, in doing so, we cannot afford to lose sight of the risk involved; the risk, that is, of destroying the social cohesion, and hence existence, of the very belief-system which we seek to 'correct', to 'purify' or to 'reform'.

Jürgen Habermas has argued that the basic concern which animates man in his historical search for survival, for life, for fulfilment, is his quest for emancipation. Man seeks liberation from everything that limits, constricts and oppresses him. Human history is the history of man's search for freedom, for salvation. This search for freedom, according to Habermas, finds threefold expression. It finds expression in the quest for control over the environment (man the worker, the natural scientist, the technologist); in man's attempts to situate him-

12 Cf. P. Fransen, 'Unity and Confessional Statements', *Bijdragen*, 33 (1972), pp. 29–30, discussing recent developments in the thought of J. B. Metz.

13 Cf. P. L. Berger, *The Social Reality of Religion* (London, 1973), pp. 38–60.

self within the linguistic, cultural tradition from which he springs (man the storyteller, the historian, the interpreter); and in his quest for some measure of wholeness, of identity, in a world of bewildering complexity, fragile meaning and endemic insecurity (man the constructor of social institutions). The human species thus secures its existence in systems of social labour and self-assertion through struggle, through tradition-bound social life in ordinary language communication, and with the aid of ego identities that at every level of individuation reconsolidate the consciousness of the individual in relation to the norms of the group.[14] Sociologically, the respective achievements of these three aspects of mankind's search for existence, and for emancipation, 'become part of the productive forces accumulated by a society, the cultural tradition through which a society interprets itself, and the legitimations that a society accepts or criticizes'.[15]

If, as I have suggested, the relationship between the Church and Jesus is fundamentally one of *anamnesis*, of remembrance, then it is clear that, of the three aspects of man's quest for freedom distinguished by Habermas, the one which most immediately concerns us here is that of the 'cultural tradition through which a society interprets itself'. Before taking up again our discussion of the structure of remembrance, however, it may be useful briefly to consider the relationship between this aspect and the other two.

The hard-won and fragile identity and security achieved by social legitimation, whether religious or secular, is itself a form of freedom – a freedom from insecurity, meaninglessness and anarchy. But the partial and particular nature of the achievement also renders it, inevitably, a form of *un*freedom. (Nowadays, we hardly need to be reminded, for example, of the ambivalence of the notion of 'law and order'.) As such, it is questioned and threatened, as I suggested earlier, by the achievements of the hermeneutical quest to liberate man from the restrictions of the present moment through the critical

14 Cf. J. Habermas, *Knowledge and Human Interests* (London, 1972), p. 313.
15 Ibid.

reappropriation of his forgotten past. In the Christian context, this task of critical reappropriation is the task of attempting, more faithfully and concretely, to 'remember Jesus'.

Thus Habermas, who remarks that 'The same configurations that drive the individual to neurosis move society to establish institutions',[16] describes the characteristic epistemological concern of the hermeneutical sciences in terms of analogies drawn from Freudian psychotherapy. The patient is 'liberated' by coming to terms with, by 'remembering', his buried past.

If we reflect, therefore, on the inevitable tension between these two distinct aspects of man's quest for freedom – freedom sought through critical interpretation of the cultural tradition and through the establishment of structures of social legitimation – it becomes clear why the Church may never become simply a revolutionary force, or simply an endorsement of the *status quo*; why it may never *simply* opt either for discontinuity, or for continuity, in relation to its past.[17] As a human *institution*, the Church seeks that form of freedom which is security, identity, order, here and now. As an *historical* people, a people constituted by the language it has inherited, the Church seeks to liberate itself from the restrictions which the past has imposed upon the present, by seeking ever more faithfully to 'hear' the message that give it birth. In the measure that it succeeds in so doing, it will discover the courage to be free for the future: to be effectively critical of its own ideological dimension, of its own institutionality, and of all other partial, particular present achievements of human freedom, individual and social.

The relationship between the task of remembrance and man's quest for freedom through instrumental knowledge and control may be more briefly stated, although it is here that confusions concerning the relationship between 'religion' and 'politics' characteristically arise.

The Christian community cannot fail to be concerned with

16 Habermas, op. cit., p. 276.
17 Cf. above, Chapter Two.

man's quest for liberation through instrumental knowledge because that community exists in order to express, embody and proclaim man's freedom in God. In so far as it is concerned with man's freedom, the Church is necessarily concerned with his freedom through work, through scientific discovery, through economic and technological development. Yet, in so far as it is concerned, not simply with this or that particular form of man's freedom, but also, beyond these particular forms, with man's total, ultimate, eschatological freedom in God, the Church will be critical of the tendency to reduce the quest for freedom to its instrumental dimension. Thus, on the one hand, the Church will proclaim man's right to work and to share in the fruits of his labour. On the other hand, it will proclaim that man does not live by bread alone.

Remembering Christ's Freedom
How is the Church to remember Jesus? Specifically, how is the Church more faithfully to remember the freedom of Christ, that freedom which the Church seeks to express, embody and proclaim in its celebration of the resurrection of Jesus Christ? In the answer to this question lies the clue to the distinctive contribution which Christians might bring to man's manifold quest for freedom. At the same time, the answer given in practice to this question will determine the stance which the Church adopts in respect of man's quest for freedom through instrumental knowledge and through social legitimations.

Our previous discussion has already ruled out one answer to this question. The tasks of faithfully remembering the freedom of Christ cannot be executed at the level of theory alone. Biblical exegesis, historical inquiry, theological reflection are certainly not unimportant, but neither are they adequate to the task. They are inadequate because, at any given period, it is precisely the unrecognized limitations and deformations, imposed on the consciousness of Christians by their history, from which they need liberation.

The form of the Church's quest to remember the freedom of

Christ cannot, then, be merely theoretical. It must be a practical form of life, and not merely a form of words. Where any relationship between individuals, or groups of individuals, is concerned, the attempt to move from mutual ignorance to mutual understanding, or from disagreement to agreement, is doomed to failure if it is restricted to a search for common statements or common concepts. If we would really understand the other person, we have to come to share the experience which determined the horizon within which his beliefs and attitudes took shape. Nor is it sufficient if the attempt to share the experience of others is restricted to an effort of the imagination. (The rich may make valiant imaginative efforts to share the experience of the poor, but this will not take them far enough.) In order to understand others, in any concreteness and depth, it is necessary in some measure to try to do what they did, to live what they lived. Only in the measure that we succeed, shall we then be able to hear what they heard, and to say what they said. Conceptual agreement is the conclusion, not the premise, of the search for understanding.

In order less inadequately to remember Christ's freedom, thus enabling his freedom to set us free, the community of the Church has to have the courage to risk doing the truth in love without waiting for the resolution of complex theoretical and hermeneutical problems.

This is not to suggest that the Church's continual attempt to remember Christ's freedom, the Church's quest to allow itself to be freed by that freedom, demands a programme of mindless activism. Responsible practice is not mindless. To question the primacy of the theoretical in the concrete enterprise of remembering the past is not to suggest that this enterprise can be undertaken without words or images. But the words and images that we use, and the way that we use them, will perhaps have more in common with the use of poetry than with the elaboration of theory. (To repeat: it is not a question of denigrating the role of theoretical reflection, but of acknowledging that it is derivative and second-order in respect of concrete living and loving, hoping and speaking.)

What is it that makes a *people,* over and above its information and practical know-how, its institutions and customs? At the deepest level there will be found a cluster of images, symbols, words and silences, in the evocation and shared use of which a people discovers and sustains its identity, its specificity, its hopes and plans.[18] This is no new insight of the sociology of knowledge; it kept the people of the old covenant alive in their celebration and their remembering or their re-living of liberation from Egypt; it keeps the people of the new covenant alive in their celebration, their remembering, their re-living of the freedom of Christ – of that act of liberation in the past which sets us free, in the present, to make our specifically Christian contribution to the promised ultimate freedom of man in the future.

If the Church is less inadequately to express, embody and proclaim the freedom of man in God, it urgently needs a deepening of that poetic consciousness which is its power to evoke and to sustain the deep symbols and silences that give it life and identity. Paradoxically, if the Church is to perform, with greater efficacy and vigour, its supportive and critical roles in respect of the instrumental and institutional aspects of human freedom, what it most deeply needs are those apparently 'useless' people, the poets and prophets who sing the songs of freedom.

It was in a context of celebration, of common worship, that Jesus evoked the people's memory of liberation in order to proclaim, in the accents of human freedom, that ultimate freedom of man in God which his life and death signified and proleptically achieved: in the synagogue, 'He stood up to read, and ... found the place where it is written: "The Spirit of the Lord is upon me.... He has appointed me to preach the good news to the poor. He has sent me to proclaim release to captives and recovery of sight to the blind, to set at liberty those who are oppressed.... Today, this scripture has been fulfilled in your hearing" '.[19]

18 Cf. P. Jacquemont, J.–P. Jossua, B. Quelquejeu, *Une Foi Exposée* (Paris, 1973), p. 121.
19 Luke iv, 17–21.

10. 'THESE THINGS WERE HERE AND BUT THE BEHOLDER WANTING'[1]

Times have changed. The insurance policy on my house declares that 'The Company shall not be liable in respect of' a number of things, including damage resulting from 'the radioactive toxic explosive or other hazardous properties of any explosive nuclear assembly or nuclear component thereof', but makes no mention of 'acts of God'. Does it follow that if damage occurred to my house such that the least implausible explanation of it was that it was attributable to an act of God, the company would pay up? Or is it simply that the insurance company has taken the risk of assuming that no event could occur of which such was the least implausible explanation?

The problem of how we are to conceive of God's action in the world is central to any account of the principal components of Christian belief. Its centrality for questions of christology, for example, has been illustrated by recent debates concerning the incarnation. And it is also central to any discussion of divine providence. In a recent paper, Brian Hebblethwaite has argued that the 'constancy' of both the 'God-world relation and the God-man relation ... is best conceived as the constancy of consistent action in the execution both of an overall purpose and of particular purposes for individual lives

---

1 From Gerard Manley Hopkins' poem 'Hurrahing in Harvest', *The Poems of Gerard Manley Hopkins,* ed. W. H. Gardner and N. H. MacKenzie (Oxford, 1970), p. 70.

within it'.[2] He goes on to point out that 'there is a tendency for the theologian ... *either* to think deistically ... *or* to fall back on the idea of miraculous intervention as the only possible kind of particular divine act within the given evolving world of nature and history'.[3]

And he rightly comments that to succumb to either of these temptations is to concede 'too much to the idea of a structured world evolving and progressing independently of its creator and sustainer'.[4]

Hebblethwaite's account draws heavily on the work of Austin Farrer. But it may, even today, also be helpful to look far further back in the history of theology. Aquinas distinguished between divine 'providence' and divine 'governance' or *gubernatio*. The distinction is between a divinely willed order or purpose in the world and its history, on the one hand, and the execution of that order or purpose, on the other. Thus, according to Aquinas, to say that all things are governed by divine providence is to say that all things have their ultimate ground in God's knowledge and love; that particular events, and the general course of events, are neither blindly fated nor anarchically, chaotically haphazard, without purpose or explanation. Aquinas' doctrine of divine providence is constructed in explicit opposition to a doctrine of mechanistic determinism, on the one hand, and to a doctrine of cosmic anarchy on the other.[5]

We shall return to this. For the time being, the thing to notice is that Aquinas' doctrine of divine providence, thus stated, says nothing about the conditions under which the occurrence of particular events, or the 'patterning' of events in general, might be *discerned* to be 'governed', or 'providentially ordered', by God's knowledge and love. And yet it is surely this which constitutes, in large part, our contemporary prob-

2 B. L. Hebblethwaite, 'Providence and Divine Action', *Religious Studies*, 14 (1978), p. 229.
3 Hebblethwaite, art, cit., p. 230.
4 Ibid.
5 Cf. Aquinas, *Summa Theologiae*, Ia, q. 22.

lem. We find it difficult to see what 'cash-value' a doctrine of providence would possess if we were unable appropriately to specify the condtions under which we might ascribe the course of events, or the occurrence of particular events, to the action of God. When a theologian says, today, that he finds the 'traditional' doctrine of divine providence naive or implausible, he is probably referring not at all to the sort of thing that Aquinas was talking about, but rather voicing a suspicion of any too hasty ascription of the occurrence of particular events to the action of God. For instance: 'We had ordered the furniture, and didn't know how we were going to pay for it, and then, out of the blue, came a five hundred pound Premium Bond win. Wasn't that providential?'

This kind of appeal to divine providence, whether in such trivial instances or on a grander scale – as in the case of certain triumphalistic accounts of the history of the Christian Church – not infrequently seems to assume that God's will coincides with ours, that his plans are our plans. Or at least, the prophetic voice that proclaims the failure of our projects, the disruption of our plans, the destruction of our cities, to be the execution of divine providence, is usually treated with hostility and suspicion.

But are these remarks not excessively superficial? Surely the Christian, the person for whom the paradigm of divine action is the Cross of Christ, knows in his heart of hearts that the pattern of divine action is unlikely closely to coincide with the patterns perceived, the projects formulated, by our limited, fearful and deeply egocentric and ethnocentric vision? True enough, but, important as this reminder may be, it throws little light on the problem of how we are appropriately to specify the conditions under which we might ascribe the course events, or the occurrence of particular events, may be ascribed to the action of God.

Whereas the so-called 'traditional' view of providence apparently finds it easy to ascribe at least some particular events to the action of God, it is increasingly common today for theologians to 'think deistically', to offer an account on which no such attempt is made. Such theologians would argue that we cannot do more than simply assert that all that occurs, that whatever occurs, is the effect of God's action, and that this action is not to be especially discerned in particular events at all.

If the first approach, while admirably trusting, too easily – and less admirably – swerves off into naiveté and superstition, the second approach, admirably recognizant of the universality of divine action, too easily – and less admirably – swerves off into a cold and irreligious agnosticism.

It is not easy to see where we go from here, for if Christian faith is neither superstitious nor agnostic, no more is it adequately characterized as some sort of compromise between the two.

It is often supposed that, of the two dangers to which I have referred – superstition and agnosticism or, perhaps, irrationalism and rationalism – it is the latter which today characteristically poses the greater threat.

That comment, by the way, is not to be taken sociologically. From a sociological point of view it is clear that we are threatened by manifold forms of irrationalism, of the flight from reason, forms of which a neurotic preoccupation with the occult and the irrationality of totalitarian *realpolitik* are only two of the most striking instances. It is also clear that many people manage to combine hard-headed rationality in their scientific or economic enterprises with forms of Christian belief that are distressingly naive, uncritical and credulous. This ability to live with religious naiveté and sophisticated secular rationality effortlessly juxtaposed would be an example of that Christian schizophrenia to which I referred in the previous essay.[6]

When I say that it is often supposed that agnosticism poses a greater threat than superstition, I have in mind the likelihood that those people who take seriously the constraints of secular rationality, and who also seek to connect the demands

6 Cf. above, Chapter Nine, p. 141.

of faith and the requirements of reason, are likely to experience the 'absence' of God as the greater threat to their religious belief.

In this essay, I want to propose the perhaps unfashionable thesis that rationalism is itself not infrequently credulous, and that credulity or superstition are not infrequently forms of unbelief. The significant contrast is not that between credulity and agnosticism but that between living by faith and living by illusory vision, between living out the conviction that 'these things were here' and any one of the manifold attempts prematurely to 'behold' them, to grasp them with imaginative or conceptual clarity.

We can begin by noticing that some doctrines of 'divine omnipresence' are perhaps more accurately described as doctrines of 'divine omniabsence'. Reacting against the view that certain types of event, or certain clusters of events, alone are to be referred to the agency of God, a doctrine of divine omnipresence retorts: No, this won't do; God is not only present and active in *some* events, he is present and active in *all* events and in all patterns of events. But this retort has often been so formulated as to imply that, because all events mediate God's action, and because God nowhere acts non-mediately, therefore our experience is exclusively of the effects of his action, and is nowhere the experience of God. Thus the concept of 'God' becomes an inference, an hypothesis, of which – depending on our personal tastes or metaphysical preferences – we may or may not decide that we have need.

And so the question arises: how is it possible for us, who live in the aftermath of that 'turn to the subject' which occurred in the seventeenth and eighteenth centuries, that shift, we might say, from the primacy of the ontological to the primacy of the epistemological, to speak of the 'experience of God'?[7]

7 In referring to 'the primacy of the epistemological', I do not intend to suggest that ontological considerations are not of fundamental significance, but simply to draw attention to the *order* in which questions of knowledge, and questions of that which is there to be known, press upon us. In all our attempts to answer the second set of questions, we

Two strategies seem to be possible. On the one hand, there are those for whom the concept of 'religious experience' stands for a discriminable psychological state, alongside such states as fear, and love, and hope, and pain. There are some psychologists of religion who would adopt such a strategy as a convenient exercise in the 'mapping' of psychological states. Such psychologists of religion will have no cause to be disturbed if some people report the absence of any such psychological state (just as some people report the absence of feelings of fear). In contrast, those philosophers of religion who accept such a notion of 'religious experience' are apt to be discomfited by the claim that this psychological state is not of universal occurrence.

Moreover, whether or not certain psychologists of religion find such a concept of 'religious experience' practically convenient, and whether or not certain philosophers of religion find if embarrassing, it raises at least two important questions for the Christian theologian. In the first place, does not this use of the concept of 'religious experience' too easily encourage those dissociations of 'secular' and 'sacred', of rationality and feeling, of matter and spirit, of knowledge of the world and knowledge of God, which have contributed so much to the supposed practical irrelevance of religious belief, by banishing religious discourse from the public places of the human quest for truth into socially marginal and obscure corners of individual private experience?

In the second place, when the concept of 'religious experience' is taken to refer to some discriminable psychological state, on what grounds is it supposed (as it frequently seems to be supposed) that such religious experience may be said to be experience of *God* in a sense that other forms of human experience – private and public, scientific and literary, domestic and political – are not? And, correlatively, on what grounds is it supposed that all experience of *God* is necessarily 'religious' in

are haunted by the first: How do we know what we are talking about? Or, to put it another way, if we are to be 'realists', we cannot today avoid the responsibility to be 'critical' realists.

the sense described? Such questions seem to be far too often glossed over by those who would adopt this first approach to the problem of our experience of God.

The second approach is characterized by the insistence that the experience of God is at least potentially, a dimension of *all* human experience – whether relational, literary, scientific, political or 'religious'. I find the distinction, drawn by Professor Charles Davis in his study *Body as Spirit*, between 'religious experience' and 'religious feeling', both valid and helpful. But, whereas Davis uses the concept of 'religious feeling' to mean 'the element in religious experience of spontaneous, connatural response to religious reality',[8] I would prefer to use the concept to refer to the element of spontaneous, connatural response to religious – that is, transcendent – reality in *all* human experience, 'secular' or 'religious'. Few modern writers have insisted more strongly on the centrality and irreducibility of man's experience of the transcendent mystery of God than Baron von Hügel. It is, therefore, all the more significant that, in answer to the question: 'Is there . . . strictly speaking, such a thing as a specifically distinct, self-sufficing, purely [religious] mode of apprehending Reality?', he should reply: 'I take it, *distinctly not.* '[9]

In similar vein, Karl Rahner insists that 'the experience of God must not be conceived of as though it were *one* particular experience *among* others. . . . The experience of God constitutes, rather . . . the ultimate depths and the radical essence of *every* spiritual and personal experience (of love, faithfulness, hope and so on)'.[10] According to this account, one dimension of *all* human experience is the experience of God whether or not we 'call the reality to which it refers "God" '.[11] It does not

8 C. Davis, *Body as Spirit* (London, 1976), p. 25
9 F. von Hügel, *The Mystical Element of Religion, Vol.II* ([2]London, 1923), p. 283 (his stress). Von Hügel has 'mystical' where I have 'religious'. In the context, however, the substitution is, I believe, faithful to his meaning.
10 K. Rahner, 'The Experience of God Today', *Theological Investigations, Vol. XI*, tr. D. Bourke (London, 1974), p. 154.
11 Ibid., p. 153.

follow that belief in God becomes irrelevant because, as Rahner says in the same essay, 'the experience itself as such can in itself be accepted more profoundly, more purely, and with greater freedom when we achieve a knowledge of its true nature and its implications at the explicitly conscious level'.[12]

Is such an approach to man's experience of God an attempt to evade the uncomfortable secularity of contemporary experience, the secularity to which Max Weber referred as 'disenchantment'? Is it, to put it crudely, an attempt to repopulate the woods with sprites, the bottom of the garden with fairies? Emphatically, no. The experience of God is always the experience of God as transcendent, as unfathomable mystery. But, in contrast to much post-Enlightenment thought, it is being urged that the mystery of God is *experienced* by man, and that 'God' is not simply the name given to a postulated entity 'outside' the world of our experience.

There is, perhaps, an analogy between our conscious and cognitive relationship with God, and our conscious and cognitive relationship with human persons. Our knowledge of other persons is never non-mediated: it is mediated by gestures and artefacts, words and silences. Nevertheless, our knowledge of other persons is *direct*, at least in the sense that we do not, or at least we do not ordinarily, *infer* their personal existence. From the fact that all our knowledge of other persons, in the mystery and transcendence of their irreducible subjectivity, is mediated, it does not follow that 'wife', 'husband' or 'friend' are simply names given to postulated entities 'outside' the world of our experience.

But, if I approach the problem of our experience and knowledge of God in terms of such an analogy am I not, in spite of my vigorous denial just now, seeking illegitimately to make habitable the cold, often brutal world of secular experience, the 'faceless' world of relentlessly impersonal 'laws' or quantifiable regularities? To give the world a 'personal face' is surely to evade the stern demands of rationality?

12 Ibid., p. 152.

This kind of criticism of religious belief has been expressed, with a rare combination of trenchancy and lucidity, by Professor Ernest Gellner.[13] Gellner is not only a philosopher, he is also a social scientist. He is far more sensitive than some professional philosophers to the sense of bewilderment, of confusion, of the absence of landmarks, that currently threatens not simply inherited modes of discourse but also inherited patterns of social organisation. If he is a rationalist, with a tendency to reduce all modes of knowledge to mechanistic explanation, his rationalism is less an expression of arrogant dogmatism than of stoic near-despair. In a situation such as ours, the only way that we can morally and intellectually *survive* is, he believes, by taking the risk of putting all our eggs in the basket of scientific rationality. Rationalism, for Gellner, is to some extent a leap in the dark, an act of faith or near-despairing hope.

According to him, ours is a society threatened on two frontiers. On the one side, there is the frontier with 'chaos', with social and cognitive anarchy. On the other side, there is the frontier with what he calls 'magical' societies. For Gellner, a 'magical' society is one that 'conflates[s] the human and the natural order, interpret[s] the one through the other and perceive[s] a kind of "meaningful unity" in reality'.[14]

Gellner's tripartite division of social cognitive strategies – the rational, the chaotic and the magical – echoes, in a most suggestive manner, the distinction, to which I referred earlier, drawn by Aquinas. Aquinas and Gellner agree that the option for anarchy, for social and cognitive chaos, is to be rejected. But whereas Aquinas also rejects a mechanistic, fatalistic account of nature and historical process, and affirms that world-process is ordered by God's purposive love, Gellner suspects all forms of religious belief of fleeing from the uninhabitably bare world of impersonal regularity disclosed by the quest for rational explanation, and of opting for the cosy, but ultimately illusory quest of the 'meaningful for us'. For Gell-

13 Cf. E. Gellner, *Legitimation of Belief* (Cambridge, 1974).
14 Gellner, op. cit., p. 26.

ner, to affirm that 'things make sense' *as a whole* and, more specifically, to affirm that the ultimate ground of reality is – in *any* sense – to be regarded as 'personal', is to see fairies in the shrubbery, gods in the garden.

Two comments are in order at this point. In the first place, Gellner's concept of a 'magical' society has much in common with that too hasty ascription of particular events to divine providential agency which which we earlier recognized as characteristic of naive, implausible and frequently superstitious forms of religious belief. I would join Professor Gellner in insisting that the bottom of the garden is inhabited by cabbages, caterpillars and grubs, and not by wood-nymphs and gods. In doing so, however, I would simply be standing in the mainstream of the Christian theological tradition, for which confession of the transcendence of the mystery of God entails the acknowledgement that God is not one particular object in the world of our experience. To confess the transcendence of the mystery of God is, amongst other things, to acknowledge that our experience and knowledge of God is mediated by those structures of particular meaning in which we order the flow of experience as we seek to discern what is, in fact, the case.

Although Professor Gellner is himself an atheist, it seems to me that his cognitive strategy is quite compatible with certain forms of deism. But, and this is my second comment, a deistic account of God's relationship with the world, and of our experience and conceptual ordering of that relationship, is not the only rational, non-credulous possibility open to us. I have suggested that it is possible to speak of man's experience of God as direct, although mediated, and to argue that all human experience is, at least potentially, ultimately experience of God, even though the conceptualization of that experience can never be such as to render the mystery of God a comprehended object of knowledge: a theology that has ceased to be insistently apophatic is either a Christmas game or else has already collapsed into idolatry.

What is at issue here, I believe, is Gellner's mistaken

identification of all forms of knowledge with *explanation.* We do seek to explain, to comprehend, to solve puzzles, to control, to put to use. There is a dimension of the human quest for meaning and truth in respect of which the model of 'problem-solving' is appropriate. Banishing, so far as possible, our preferences, tastes, evaluative assessments and personal commitments (save only the commitment to truth), we seek to discover what is the case. Our commitments, our policies for action, wait upon the results of that quest. Here, theory precedes practice, knowledge precedes commitment (even though it is our previous practice and prior commitments which shape the manner in which we pursue the theoretical quest). This is the dimension of human inquiry which we perhaps tend to associate with the natural sciences and their related technologies or 'practical applications'.

But there is another dimension of the human quest for meaning and truth in respect of which 'understanding', rather than 'explanation', 'interpretation' rather than 'control', is our objective. Where our knowledge of other persons is concerned, although it is true to say that we cannot love somebody whom we have never met, or of whom we have never heard, nevertheless it remains the case that, really to 'get to know' another person, we have to take the risk of friendship, of commitment, of love. Here, knowledge is the fruit, rather than the precondition of commitment. And it is not only in respect of our relationship with other human individuals that the model of loving attention, of contemplative wonder, is more appropriate than the model of explanation and control. Something similar is the case where those forms of the quest for truth characteristic of, for example, the poet, the artist or the novelist are concerned.

I am vastly oversimplifying exceedingly complex issues.[15] I

15 Thus, for example, I would wish to maintain that an insistence on the irreducibility of the distinction which I am drawing here between 'cognitive strategies' is quite compatible with the view that there are 'family resemblances' between types of *theory* construction in the natural and hermeneutical sciences. Cf. my review article of Pannenberg's *Theology and the Philosophy of Science* in the *Clergy Review*, lxii (1977), pp. 158–61.

do so simply in order to suggest that there are irreducibly distinct modes of knowledge, and that the decision as to which mode of knowledge is appropriate, in particular instances, will depend upon what it is that we seek to know and understand, and the point of view from which, in any particular inquiry, we seek to understand it. The objects of inquiry, and the aspects under which they are, in particular instances, objects of inquiry, decide the appropriate forms of the quest for meaning and truth. However, even if such considerations are important, and are too often neglected, are they perhaps only relevant in respect of our choice of cognitive strategies in particular instances? Or are they also relevant in respect of our overall cognitive strategy, in respect of what we might call our total way of being in the world?

Here we have to be very careful, because it is not at all clear that we can legitimately make the move from speaking about meaning *in* the world (and about the diverse forms of the human quest for meaning in the world) to speaking about the meaning *of* the world. How are we, with our limited experience and understanding, our personal and cultural limitations and blindnesses, to speak with any confidence of 'the meaning of the world'? Perhaps we should not do so. And yet, it seems to me that those of us who have been led, by reflection on our history and experience, to confess our faith in the God of Christian belief, a God who is Lord of nature and history alike, are constrained to affirm that the world *has* meaning and purpose being, as it is, the expression of God's purposive governance.

And it is here, perhaps, that some of the fundamental divisions between Christian believers begin to emerge. There are those who not only affirm that the world has meaning and purpose, but who also affirm that this meaning and purpose may be more or less straightforwardly discerned, grasped, 'read off' our individual or group experience. I have already indicated my belief that such a stance tends towards credulity, superstition and illusion. Its mistake: it moves too swiftly from the affirmation that 'these things were here' to the affirmation that they are here for the beholding; it seeks, prematurely, to live by sight.

But it is to be noticed that the attempt prematurely to live by sight is equally characteristic of the kind of reductionist scientism, be it atheist or agnostic in respect of religious reality, which, identifying 'knowledge' with 'explanation', is impatient of those forms of the quest for knowledge which seek, not to grasp, but to attend, not to control, but wonderingly to respect the incomprehensibility of the mystery they contemplate.

There are also those, however, who, while affirming that the world has meaning and purpose, deny that this meaning and purpose may – whether in respect of particular events or of large-scale patterns in human history – be straightforwardly discerned, grasped, or 'read off' our individual or group experience. The crucial word there is 'straightforwardly'. And if some such fundamental stance in respect of meaning and purpose is characteristic of certain forms of agnosticism and even atheism, it is also, I suggest, characteristic of those forms of Christian belief which take with full seriousness the implications of the claim that Good Friday is the place of revelation, that the paradigm of divine action in the world is the passion of the Lord's anointed.

This leads me to a final step in the argument. I have spoken of 'contemplation', of 'attentiveness', of the respect for mystery. Am I suggesting that the appropriate stance of the Christian in the world is fundamentally inactive; that the Christian, instead of seeking to 'change the world', should be stoically content with the attempt to 'understand' it?[16] By no means. It may be true that, in order to get to know other human persons, we have to attend, rather than control; that human beings are mysteries to be respected, not problems energetically to be licked. Nevertheless, the way to the knowledge of other persons is, in practice, always a way of demanding and costly engagement, a way of suffering, of compassion. There is

16 Here I have in mind Marx's critique of Feuerbach's 'contemplativity'.

an irreducible variety in the modes of human action, as there is the modes of human knowledge. In personal relationships, knowledge is the fruit, and not merely the precondition, of engagement, of suffering, of love. What I am suggesting is that perhaps one of the reasons that we characterize the transcendent mystery of God as 'personal' is because we have discovered that the process of 'coming to know' God, and of discerning his action in the world, has a similar structure.

I have attempted, in this essay, to follow the lines of Aquinas' approach to the problem of divine providence in urging that a doctrine of providence stands in opposition to a doctrine of mechanistic determinism, on the one hand, and to a doctrine of cosmic anarchy, on the other, but to do so in a manner that respects our modern preference for approaching such problems phenomenologically and epistemologically, rather than through consideration of questions of formal ontology.

'These things were here and but the beholder wanting.' I take it that the denial that 'these things were here' is incompatible with any coherent doctrine of divine providence. I have been trying to suggest, however, that it may make sense to affirm that 'these things were here', while at the same time acknowledging that the constraints of human, historical existence are such that, in any straightforward sense, the 'beholder is wanting', and that to seek prematurely to 'behold' is to substitute credulity for faith.

And yet, as the fourth gospel is fond of reminding us, there may be another, fragile, paradoxical, supremely significant sense in which we, who live and work in the darkness of faith, may even now be said to be beholders of the action of God.

11. ETERNAL LIFE: LIFE 'AFTER' DEATH?[1]

'Immortality' or 'Resurrection'?
Professor Maurice Wiles has questioned the legitimacy of the
fashionable contention that, firstly, there is a deep conceptual
gulf between the notions of 'immortality' and 'resurrection'
and, secondly, that 'the early church is warmly [to be] com-
mended for preferring the resurrection of the body to the
immortality of the soul as the way of expressing its belief in a
life beyond death'.[2] He prefers to soften the contrast between
the two notions by pointing out that, since human existence is,
in its inception and continuation, wholly the gift of God, the
immortality of the soul is in no sense a matter of man's own
achievement. Therefore, belief in immortality does not involve
any ' "Pelagian" derogation from the grace of God'.[3]

His argument is, I believe, theoretically sound but existen-
tially wide of the mark. We are afraid to die; we are afraid of
that erosion, that crumbling into chaos, which is death the
unknown as it threatens us. If we can convince ourselves that
some constituent element of our present personal existence is

1 This essay was first published in the *Heythrop Journal*, xix (1978), pp.
271–84. It provoked an interesting response from Brian Hebblethwaite,
on which I briefly commented (for both pieces, cf. *Heythrop Journal*, xx
[1979], pp. 57-64). Although I found many of his detailed criticisms
both perceptive and helpful, I still wish to stand by the substance of my
argument. I have therefore left the text unchanged, indicating in the
notes some of the principal points that were made in the subsequent
discussion.
2 M. F. Wiles, *The Remaking of Christian Doctrine* (London, 1974), p. 126.
3 Wiles, op. cit., p. 129.

indestructible, we can in some measure evade the deadliness and finality of death. We may give 'notional assent' to the fact that this indestructible element is only such in view of God's unswerving creative love and fidelity but, where our 'real assents' are concerned, the conviction that our 'soul' cannot die is a surer bulwark against panic than is our wavering trust that, across the dissolution of death, God will raise us up. A soul in the hand is worth two in the eschaton!

In other words, although, from the standpoint of Christian belief, the notions of 'immortality' and 'resurrection' may be theoretically less mutually incompatible than the fashionable contrast between them would suggest, a preference for the model of 'immortality' may, in practice, serve as yet another device enabling us to refuse to die. Such a refusal is often not lacking in courage and nobility. Socrates believed in the immortality of the soul and, as Eberhard Jüngel says, 'he greeted death with a swan-song'. But Jüngel goes on: 'When Jesus died he uttered a cry. The swan-song announced the return to God. Jesus cried: "My God, my God, why hast thou forsaken me?" ... And yet it is precisely the death of Jesus which is proclaimed as salvation.'[4] Does not this suggest that the heroic 'Non moriar' may be dangerously close to the destructively egocentric 'Non serviam'? We shall return to this.

It is not my intention, in this essay, further to explore the contrast, or supposed contrast, between the notions of 'immortality' and 'resurrection'. Both of these notions are used to express the relationship between this life and life 'after' death. It is this 'after' that puzzles me. Is it not perhaps the case that, whichever of the two models we use to express that relationship, the conviction that there is life 'after' death may serve as yet another evasion of the finality of death? To put it as starkly and paradoxically as possible, I propose to argue that belief in resurrection is compatible with disbelief in life 'after' death.

---

4 E. Jüngel, *Death: The Riddle and the Mystery* (Edinburgh, 1975), p. 53.

John Hick on 'Recapitulation'
Professor John Hick would, I suspect, classify the suggestion
that I am putting forward as an instance of what he calls
'recapitulation theories'; that is, theories which 'suggest that
man's immortality is the eternal presence of his earthly life
within the divine memory'.[5] (If I am reluctant to accept such
classification, this is partly because I find the concept of God
'remembering' as puzzling as I would that of God 'predict-
ing'.) Hick maintains that, although such a view was first put
forward by the 'very individual Spanish catholic writer
Miguel de Unamuno', and has become 'the most distinctive
new protestant thinking about the last things', it 'was not
taken up within catholic thought'.[6] That he can make this
latter claim is perhaps explained by the fact that his examination of Rahner's thought on these matters is almost entirely
restricted to the highly speculative monograph *On the Theology
of Death*, and takes no account of Rahner's studies of the resurrection or of the interpretation of eschatological assertions.
But this, in turn, is perhaps not surprising in view of the
extremely sketchy character of Hick's treatment of the resurrection of Christ,[7] and the complete neglect, in his chapter on
'Later Christian Thought', of the christological dimension of
such thought, as if reflection on the death and resurrection of
Jesus had no influence on Christian concepts of 'eternal life'.[8]

    Hick would, I imagine, level against my modest proposal
objections similar to those which he levels against that form of
the 'recapitulation theory' propounded by Wolfhart Pannenberg.[9] This would not greatly distress me, for two reasons. In
the first place, several of these objections seem principally to
arise from the fact that Hick's concept of God is heavily anthro-
pomorphic in a quite specific sense: God is spoken of as

5   J. Hick, *Death and Eternal Life* (London, 1976), p. 215.
6   Loc. cit.
7   Cf. Hick, pp. 171–81.
8   In contrast, Rahner insists that 'Anything that cannot be read and
    understood as a christological assertion is not a genuine eschatological
    assertion', *Theological Investigations*, Vol. IV (London, 1966), p. 343.
9   Cf. Hick, pp. 221–7.

'seeing' or 'knowing' in the 'spectatorial' sense in which human beings who undergo or, as Aquinas would have said, 'suffer' their conscious experience, are sometimes said to 'see' or 'know'. Hick's God does not at any point seem to be a God of whom it could intelligibly be said: *scientia Dei causa rerum*.

In the second place, Hick informs us that 'the metaphorical or symbolic character of eschatological language' does not entitle us to refrain from giving 'literal and not metaphorical answers' to questions concerning 'when and where the indescribable experience of participating in God's vision of our earthly lives takes place'.[10] Frankly, I have no idea as to what would count as 'literal and not metaphorical answers' to questions concerning postulated spatio-temporal characteristics of eternal life.

Metaphors of Eternity

That time-talk, temporality, succession, before-and-after, are only directly and literally appropriate in respect of historical process, is not a very controversial suggestion. Once accepted, it follows that to speak of God's existence in time-talk terms is to speak metaphorically. It may be that we are obliged to use such metaphors: language itself has an inbuilt successiveness; there is no language than can adequately speak of eternity. Or, rather, there is only one Word in which the simultaneity of God's eternity is adequately and non-successively expressed, and that Word is consubstantial with the Father, which we are not.

Nevertheless, even if we are obliged to use metaphors of time to speak of God's eternity, we should at least find such usage puzzling, unsatisfying, bewildering. And yet do we not sometimes speak with disturbing ease, and absence of bewilderment, of God's existence as if it were a sort of 'parallel time-track' to historical process?

Or consider the notion of 'pre-existence'. We know that we

10 Hick, p. 224.

did not exist before we began to be. And that 'beginning to be' is, for each of us, a datable event in time. Happy birthday to you! You did not exist when you were but a twinkle in your father's eye. But do we not want to say that there is a sense in which we were, each of us, from all eternity (if I may be permitted the metaphor) a twinkle in our heavenly Father's eye? By all means, but any talk of the 'eternal pre-existence' of the human individual is presumably an attempt to express our total dependence on the timeless creative care of God. If I were to say that each human individual exists, in God, from all eternity, before all time, I would not be taken to be denying, or qualifying, the non-metaphorical assertion that each human existence has a beginning, and that it has its beginning in time, and that before it began to be it did not exist. (Something similar presumably applies to our handling of the notion of the 'pre-existence' of Jesus the Christ, the Word made flesh, but to explore this would take me too far from the theme of this essay.)

History has a beginning and an end. Each individual human existence has a beginning. Each individual human existence has also an end. If talk of 'pre-existence' is metaphorical, if it would be incorrect to suppose that such talk denies, or qualifies the simple assertion that there was a time when each of us was not, why should not the same considerations apply to talk of 'post-existence'? Each individual human existence has an end. We are born, we come into being; we die, we cease to be. To speak about life 'after' death is to speak metaphorically. It is no more literally true to say that, after death, we continue to exist, than it is to say that, before we were born, we pre-existed. If talk of the eternal pre-existence of the human individual is an attempt to express our total dependence on the timeless creative care of God, perhaps talk of life 'after' death is, similarly, an attempt to express the permanence of our dependence on the timeless creative and redemptive care of God.[11] God lives, and God's love creates

11 I am not here, as Hebblethwaite maintains, *assimilating* 'resurrection-

the objects of his love, objects which, as contingent, have their existence temporally and successively, but which yet ceaselessly exist in the timeless moment of God's eternity.

Earlier in this essay, I referred to the disturbing ease with which we sometimes speak of God's timeless, non-successive existence as if it were a sort of parallel time-track to historical process. And, when we do so, we sometimes speak as if, at death, we 'jumped the tracks' or 'changed horses',[12] and continued to exist on God's parallel time-track. But this is the language of myth or, I would prefer to say in this context, of metaphor. If we fail continually to advert to the metaphorical status of such discourse we are in danger both of evading the reality, the finality of death, and of taking with insufficient seriousness the constituent moments of our temporal existence.

In saying this, I have in mind, for example, the dubious propriety of a not uncommon form of popular preaching. Most of us are familiar with those awful warnings lest, in a state of enmity with God, our life is suddenly and unexpectedly cut short. Repent: how dreadful it would be if death struck swiftly

---

talk' to 'pre-existence' talk (p. 60). However, while wishing to maintain that there are analogies to be drawn between the two set of metaphors, I admit that the limits of such analogies need to be more carefully drawn.

12 The latter image, according to Rahner, is derived from Feuerbach. Professor Stephen Sykes describes Rahner's own proposal to speak of eternal life, in contrast, as 'something radically withdrawn from the former temporal dimension', as 'far from clear'. But what sort of clarity should we expect in these matters? Sykes himself maintains that 'in order to provide minimum conditions of intelligibility for the doctrines of a resurrection to judgement and of the enjoyment of heaven, which it will be argued are integral to a coherent Christian theology, the term "life" will inevitably carry temporal connotations which cannot be thought away in some a-temporal conceptuality'. I share his positive concern, but does not his manner of expressing it tend to confuse the intelligible with the imaginable (to be, as Lonergan would say, 'counterpositional') and thus to sidestep the considerations with which I am concerned in this essay? Cf. Rahner, *Theological Investigations*, Vol. XIII (London, 1975), p. 174; S. W. Sykes, 'Life After Death: the Christian Doctrine of Heaven', in *Creation, Christ and Culture*, ed. R. W. A. McKinney (Edinburgh, 1976), pp. 251–2.

in your sleep, before you could turn again to God. The implication is that only the final instants of historical existence are of ultimate ethical and theological significance; that those final instances fix and eternally determine the individual's relationship with God. In terms of the image of the 'two tracks', such preaching presumes that, in that state in which we 'jump the tracks', we inexorably and eternally *are*. And that presumption, in turn, rests upon a model of the relationship between historical existence and eternal life according to which the latter is envisaged as temporally succeeding the former: eternal life takes over where historical existence leaves off.

However, in the measure that only the final instants of our life are regarded as of ultimate significance for the form and quality of our eternal relationship with God, the whole of our previous history is correspondingly deprived of ultimate significance. And if that previous history is deprived of ultimate significance, it is also deprived of ultimate reality: as we move into death, our past has simply ceased to be, it has slipped out of existence, save as memory and as that which went to shape our end. But can this be quite right? Can any contingent expression of God's timeless life and love simply cease to be? Is there not a sense in which everything that is, is eternally, in so far as it is an expression of the being of God? Karl Barth says of 'past time': 'because God was then, it was real and full time. And because God was then, its reality and fullness cannot be taken away by the fact that it has gone. . . . What He has once given He does not take back again. What was by Him and before Him still is.'[13]

A relationship between two human beings has its ups and downs, its moments of ecstasy and moments of betrayal. So long as that relationship endures, we seek to improve its quality. But we do not say of a marriage, for example, that all that really matters is how it ended. Or, if we were so to speak, would we not be intolerably trivializing the pain and joy, the

13 K. Barth, *Church Dogmatics*, *III/2* (Edinburgh, 1960), p. 537.

expectation and responsibility, of each particular moment in that temporally structured relationship?

Some Theologians on the Finality of Death

Each individual existence, each relationship, each pattern of relationships, each language, each society, has a beginning, and it also has an end. All temporal reality begins to be, endures and ceases to be. There is no time 'before' time. There is no time 'after' time. We did not exist before we began to be. We shall no longer exist after we have died. If we are to find meaning in the notion of 'eternal life', we must seek it in the relationship between historical existence and God's eternity, not in some 'other' existence, subsequent to and conceived on the model of historical time.

A number of modern theologians, while attempting to take seriously the finality of death, seem to draw back, to pull their punches, at the last moment. Jüngel, for example, says that: 'Although it frequently has been and will be interpreted in this way, the hope of resurrection cannot involve the expectation that life's temporal limitations will be dissolved.'[14] There is a significant hesitancy in the phrase 'life's temporal limitations'. Again: 'God's creative relationship to man excludes the possibility that this relationship can be broken, but it does not exclude the fact that human life comes to an end.'[15] But then he goes on: 'Beyond that which has come to an end there is not simply nothing, but the same God who was in the beginning.'[16] I am not sure whether or not I agree with this, because I am not at all clear what he is trying to say.

There is a similar ambiguity in Moltmann's *The Crucified God*: '"Resurrection of the dead"', he says, 'excludes any idea of a "life after death" ... whether in the idea of the immortality of the soul or in the idea of the transmigration of souls. Resurrection life is not a further life after death, whether in the

14 Jüngel, op. cit., p. 119.
15 Jüngel, p. 90.
16 Loc. cit.

soul or the spirit, in children or in reputation; it means the annihilation of death in the victory of the new, eternal life.'[17]

Barth devotes a section of the *Church Dogmatics* to the theme of 'Man in His Time', and he says of its final subsection, 'Ending Time', that it embodies a 'view of human nature, with its frank recognition of the fact that it ends as well as begins'.[18] This sounds promising, as do phrases such as the following: 'When we die, all things and we ourselves come to an end';[19] 'Whatever existence in death may mean, it cannot consist in a continuation of life in time. One day we shall have had our life.'[20] And again: 'An end is set to our time. One day our life will cease to be. Death is a reality.'[21] 'One day we shall cease to be, but even then He will be for us. Hence our future non-existence cannot be our complete negation.'[22]

We seem to be getting stuck. Christian speech concerning the mystery of death, and man's participation in the eternal life of God, takes its shape and structure from our attempts to understand that which faith compels us to say concerning the fate of Jesus. It is faith in Christ's resurrection that leads theologians such as Jüngel, Moltmann and Barth to speak as they do of man's death. It may help, therefore, if we turn our attention to questions such as the following: When we confess Christ as risen, does that confession entail the belief that, subsequent to his death, he moved into another order of continuing existence? Or is belief in Christ's resurrection compatible with a denial that, at death, Jesus 'jumped the tracks'? Are the only alternatives open to us either the affirmation that, at death, Jesus 'jumped the tracks', or the affirmation that he lives only in the sense that his memory is kept alive amongst us?

The latter view is not one that is associated with either Karl

17 J. Moltmann, *The Crucified God* (London, 1974), p. 170.
18 Barth, *Church Dogmatics, III/2*, p. 633.
19 Ibid., p. 588.
20 Ibid., p. 589.
21 Ibid., p. 594.
22 Ibid., p. 611.

Barth or Karl Rahner. Yet both Barth and Rahner seem reluctant to be stuck on the other prong of my Morton's fork! Barth says of the resurrection and ascension that they 'add to what He was and is and to what took place in Him ... only the new fact that in this event He was to be seen and was actually seen as the One He was and is. He did not become different in this event ... His resurrection and ascension were simply the authentic communication and proclamation of the perfect act of redemption once for all accomplished in his previous existence and history'.[23] And again, in the following volume: 'The radically new thing in the coming again of the man Jesus who obviously died on the Cross was not a prolongation of his existence terminated by death like that of every other man, but the appearance of his terminated existence in its participation in the sovereign life of God.'[24] The clearest statement of Barth's that I know occurs in a letter which he wrote in 1961: 'Eternal life is not another, second life beyond our present one, but the reverse side of *this* life, as God sees it, which is hidden from us here and now. It is this life in relationship to what God has done in Jesus Christ for the whole world and also for us. So we wait and hope – in respect of our death – to be made *manifest* with him (Jesus Christ who is raised from the dead).'[25]

'He did not become different in this event.' In the same direction, and rather more succinctly, Rahner says that 'the resurrection of Christ is not another event *after* his passion and death ... the resurrection is the manifestation of what happened in the death of Christ'.[26] This is all of a piece with Rahner's insistence that Christian faith 'takes seriously the fact that this life is one and single, and is brought to its fulness in a single and definitive historical development'.[27] Or, as he

23 Barth, *Church Dogmatics*, *IV/2* (Edinburgh, 1958), p. 133.
24 Barth, *Church Dogmatics*, *IV/3* (Edinburgh, 1961), p. 312.
25 E. Busch, *Karl Barth* (London, 1976), p. 488. Hebblethwaite points out that Barth's 'words are designed to rule out the possible relevance of parapsychology to the question of eternal life' (pp. 57-8).
26 K. Rahner, *Theological Investigations*, Vol. IV (London, 1966), p. 128.
27 Rahner, *Theological Investigations*, Vol. XIII (London, 1975), p. 174.

puts it elsewhere: those who have died 'do not prolong their existence in a different life'.[28]

Walter Kasper's lucid treatment of 'the content of faith in Jesus' resurrection' closely follows Rahner. Unfortunately, however, although the discussion begins with an admirable insistence on the metaphorical status of the concept of resurrection, Kasper seems insufficiently attentive to the need critically to appropriate the significance of the fact that uses of the notion of 'subsequence', in this context, are similarly metaphorical.[29] I suggest that the clue to be picked up from this discussion is that the profitable question to be asking is not so much: What happens *after* death? but rather: What happens *in* death?

Living and Dying

I began by suggesting that the failure sufficiently to advert to the metaphorical status of all talk of life 'after' death is facilitated by our deep-seated reluctance to face up to the fact of the finality of death. In the previous section I have been suggesting, with the help of Barth and Rahner, that it is misleading to speak of 'resurrection' as another state of affairs, or event, subsequent to death, or of 'risen life' as a prolongation, in however new a form, of temporal existence. I would now like to push the problem one stage further by asking the question: Is 'dying' a process subsequent to 'living'? Do we first 'live' and then 'die'? There is a trivial sense in which the answer can only be 'Yes': namely, that a person can only cease to be if he has previously come into existence. But is that the end of the matter?

At death, our bodily existence is terminated. But what do we mean by our 'body'? My body is not simply this lump of matter by means of which I communicate with other people. My body is also the world constituted by the personal, social and economic relationships in which I share. These all form

28 Ibid., p. 196.
29 Cf. W. Kasper, *Jesus the Christ* (London, 1976), pp. 144–54.

part of me. My language, my family, my city, are parts of my body. When I die, it is not merely this lump of matter that dies: the whole network of personal, family and social communications of which I formed a part, dies a little too. It therefore follows that the process of dying starts much earlier than the moment of terminal death. It is not only at the moment of terminal death that our world, our body, dies. Just as the physical constituents that go to make up this lump of matter are changing all the time – cells being replaced, hair and teeth dropping out – so also the network of relationships and communication that constitutes our body, in the wider sense, is changing all the time. And here, too, the changes that occur often amount to irretrievable loss. I am not just thinking of the death of friends and loved ones. I am also thinking of what happens when you change your job or place of residence. Close friendships turn into Christmas-card contacts, and wither away. Quite often, to return in nostalgic expectation to a place in which one once experienced great happiness is poignantly to discover the irrecoverability of the past. More seriously, by our failure to communicate, to know and to care, by our blindness and betrayal, we contribute daily to each other's dying. Dying is not just something that takes place during our last few weeks or hours. Just as our physical bodies, from the moment when they leave the womb, are set on a journey which leads, inexorably and ever more obviously, to senility and decay, so also it is true of the whole of our temporal existence that the process of living is *also* the process of dying. They are not *two* processes that succeed one another.

We can get at least one step further, I think, without bending our language too far. There seems to be a sense in which, without the willingness to die, human existence remains mere 'existence' and cannot flourish, cannot 'come alive'. In our relationships with other people, with new ideas and the challenge of fresh situations, we have continuously to be risking the unknown, the unfamiliar, the disturbing. We have to risk the destruction of whatever 'safe little world' we have so far succeeded in carving out of chaos. The person who has not the courage thus to risk 'dying', throughout his life, is unlikely to have the courage to die at the end. The person who has not the courage to live for other people, the courage to risk the unknown, the courage to risk relationship – and thereby to risk the 'death' of separation or betrayal – will not have the courage to die into the arms of God. The person who tries to live 'privately', to hang on to his possessions, his friendships, his certainties, will die 'privately', alone, and this is hell. As Karl Rahner puts it: 'mortal sin consists in the will to die autonomously'.[30]

Two Stories of Man

What has all this got to do with the status of the notion of life 'after' death? I have been suggesting that 'living' and 'dying' should be considered not so much as successive stages in our historical existence, but rather as two dimensions of one single process that demands to be thus doubly described. Perhaps 'two dimensions' is wrong: the spatial metaphor is unhelpful here. Instead, let us say that our historical existence is such that two accounts have to be given of it, two stories told. On one account, our historical existence is a process of living or, rather, of 'coming alive'. On the other account, it is a process of dying; a process of ceasing to be. And if, in certain situations, the 'Yes' of life seems 'obviously' to be the dominant description, muting the 'No' of death, and vice versa, we should remember that it is imprudent overconfidently to assert that this, the way things seem at the moment to be, is how things truly are, in the sight of God. (The warning note that I have just sounded has plentiful precedent in Christian tradition: in the reminder, for example, that the Christian may never roundly assert how it is that he stands before God, and in the Church's ability to sing, in her Easter liturgy, of the *felix culpa*.)

Nevertheless, there does seem to be a fundamental asym-

---

30 Rahner, *On the Theology of Death* (London, 1961), p. 52.

metry between the two stories. To tell the story of our historical existence as a tale of our dying requires only honesty,
realism and courage. What would be necessary for us to be
able, without retracting this first account, also to tell the story
– the *whole* story, including the story of terminal death – as a
tale of our coming alive?

So far, my suggestion that the single process of human existence should be doubly described, as the story of dying and as
the story of coming alive, has involved virtually no recourse to
theological considerations. It has been little more than an
exercise in phenomenology, or impressionistic anthropology.
And, as such, it will not work, because it seems impossible
thus doubly to describe terminal death. And this impossibility
surely threatens the validity of *all* our talk of 'coming alive'? It
will have been noticed, however, that my suggestion bears
some resemblance to the two accounts which Barth gives of
the history of Jesus. He first tells that story as a tale of the 'way
of the Son of God into the far country',[31] and then as a tale of
the 'homecoming of the Son of Man'.[32] But, although the tales
have to be consecutively told (because we cannot say everything at once), he insists that they are not tales of two consecutive histories, one of which begins at the point at which the
other leaves off. It is not that Jesus first trod the way of the Son
of God into the far country and then, subsequently, underwent
a second journey, the journey of the homecoming of the Son of
Man. Rather, there is *one* history of Jesus Christ, which must
be told two ways. But, and this is why my anthropological
sketch ran into difficulties, the second way of telling the story
is only possible from the standpoint of Easter faith.

I have been insisting, from the outset, that we take seriously
the reality, the finality, of death. To speak from Easter faith is
in no way an entitlement to substitute the second way of telling the story for the first. It is in no way an entitlement to
claim that the first way of telling the story can be dispensed
with, that it is not 'really' true. There must be no question of

31 Barth, *Church Dogmatics*, *IV/1* (Edinburgh, 1956), pp. 157–210.
32 Barth, *Church Dogmatics*, *IV/2*, pp. 20–154.

pretending that the journey into the far country did not 're-ally' take place, of pretending that it was illusory. It was not. That first way of telling the story tells the truth: suffering, loneliness, alienation and death were not illusions for the Christ, any more than they are for any of us.

I suggested earlier that the question we should be asking is not so much: What happens 'after' death? but rather: What happens *in* death? Supposing that, in death, in dying, Jesus discovers that his whole history, and every moment in that history, far from slipping away, ephemeral, into nonexistence, *stands*, eternally – and stands with the transfigured reality and significance which belong to it from the standpoint of God's eternal light? And supposing that, having gone to the furthest limits of the far country and discovered himself *there* (and not somewhere else) to be at home with his Father, he is able, in the gift of his Spirit, to share that discovery with us?

I am suggesting, in other words, that the concept of 'risen life' be taken to refer, not to another order of existence subse-quent to that which we historically experience, but to that single historical process, with its beginning and its end defining and delimiting its particularity, as experienced from the standpoint of the God who, in the stillness of unchanging love, creates, sustains and enlivens that process.[33] To say that

33 Hebblethwaite doubts whether 'all this talk', by Barth, Jüngel, Rahner and myself, of 'timeless participation in the glory of God makes very much sense' (p. 61; in fact, I have avoided speaking of 'timeless partici-pation in the glory of God', preferring to speak of man's participation in God's timeless glory), and he adduces christological and soteriological reasons for preferring to retain a 'subsequence' model of the relation of time to eternity. However, his principal charge against my position is that, unlike Barth, Jüngel and Rahner ('It is just possible to accept that for them "God is not the God of the dead but of the living" ', p. 60), I am a latter-day Sadducee, and he offers the sentence to which this note is attached as evidence for the prosecution. He maintains that, on my account, '*We* drop out of the picture' (p. 60). But this is impossible. If, on *my* account, we 'drop out of the picture', we were never in it in the first place! Perhaps my meaning might have been clearer if I had said: 'as experienced *by us* from the standpoint of God'. Had I done so he would, I think, have acquitted me of the charge of Saduceeism. Moreover, just as it is inevitable that we, who live in time and history,

life, in Christ, is eternal, is not to say that it has no beginning
and no end but that even in its finitude and particularity it is,
as finite and particular, eternally an expression of God, a participation in his eternity, although the irreversible recognition
that this is the case cannot precede its historical achievement,
in death. Where the paradox of 'death as resurrection' is concerned, we need to bear in mind what Karl Rahner has called
'the axiom of all relationship between God and creature,
namely that the closeness and the distance, the submissiveness
and the independence of the creature do not grow in inverse
but in like proportion'.[34] Hence that which seems prospec-
tively to be the dissolution of our 'real' existence is, in fact, its
achievement. We have already seen that this is provisionally,
proleptically experienced in the 'risk-laden' nature of all relationship.

Three Objections

This whole laborious exercise has been little more than an
invitation to reconsider the model in terms of which we conceive of the relationship between historical existence and the
eternity of God. By way of conclusion, I would like briefly to
comment on three possible objections.

---

should 'picture' the divine existence in quasi-temporal, successive
terms, so also it is inevitable that we should similarly 'picture' the
participation in God's eternity of those who have died. Our temporal
relationship to those who historically precede or succeed us imposes
certain imaginative and grammatical constraints. Nevertheless. even if
we have little alternative but to say that Jesus (or any other person who
'once died') 'now lives' in God, it is only to the extent that we lose sight
of the *metaphorical* component in such a statement that it appears to
contradict the argument of this essay, which is, after all, little more than
a modest exercise in what used to be called the metaphysics of partici-
pated being.

34 Rahner, *Theological Investigations*, Vol. IV, p. 117. This principle, implied
in Barth's 'two stories', is spelt out in its christological and trinitarian
implications in D. M. MacKinnon, 'The Relation of the Doctrines of the
Incarnation and the Trinity', in *Creation, Christ and Culture* (n. 12 above),
pp. 92–107.

In the first place, if all such talk is, as I insisted at the beginning, inevitably metaphorical, what benefit is to be gained by seeking to replace one model, one set of metaphors, by another? What advantage has the model that I have been trying to sketch over the apparently more straightforward model of a subsequent mode of continuing existence? I suggest that the answer is that, by inhibiting us from talking about 'another' life, a life 'after' this one, it might help us to take more seriously the responsibilities of our historical existence. If 'eternal life' is *this* life, experience not in 'successiveness' but in 'simultaneity',[35] then there is no justification for the view that this life is simply to be endured, or tolerated, while awaiting a compensatory 'life to come'.

Christian faith, far from functioning as a narcotic, should profoundly stimulate its adherents to take, not simply the historical process as a whole (which is the tendency of Marxism), but also each and every aspect and feature of that process, each moment, each relationship, each person, with utmost seriousness. Events in time *matter*, if the temporal is the contingent form, and not simply the antechamber, of the eternal.

The second objection would question whether my model leaves sufficient room for the forgiveness of sin. It is all very well to say of Christ that, in death, he discovers his whole historical existence eternally to stand. But surely we would not want this? It would, says Rahner, 'be terrible if our former life, with all its banalities and questionable aspects were itself to be frozen in a final and definitive state'.[36] He answers, rather sharply, with a warning against 'mythological fantasizing', adding: 'the definitive state of our former life in its historical development is far from implying a petrification of its former banalities and questionable factors'.[37] The warning is timely, but I am not convinced that his reply really meets the objec-

---

35 The categories, of course, are von Hügel's. He would, I think, have approved of some, but not all, of the ideas in this essay. Cf. F. von Hügel, *Eternal Life* (London, 1913).
36 Rahner, *Theological Investigations*, Vol. XIII, p. 174.
37 Loc. cit.

tion. I think we must see if there is not something more that we can say.

In the first place, it would surely be most unbiblical, and untraditional, to contend that God's forgiveness of man's sin, the transformation of man's egocentricity by the grace of God's transformative self-donation, occurs exclusively 'after' death. If grace is the 'beginning of glory', then it is not the forgiveness of sin for which my model does not (apparently) sufficiently allow, but the definitive achievement of that forgiveness in man's glorification. In the second place, however, if my account of resurrection is plausible, then I have in fact sufficiently allowed for the fact of man's glorification, even if I have not succeeded in offering any imaginatively satisfying account of this. In the third place, I suggest that we should be suspicious of imaginatively satisfying accounts. The attempts to provide such accounts have usually not been free from an element of 'mythological fantasy'.

Nevertheless, I will tentatively risk a simple analogy. Suppose a relationship between two human beings, one of whom loves with unswerving fidelity and generosity, while the other vacillates between answering love, insensitivity and betrayal. A crisis occurs in the relationship, such that the unfaithful lover suddenly sees the quality of the other's love. In such recognition, it is not unthinkable that pain and remorse should be overwhelmed by the joyful realisation that it was ceaseless faithful love that was ultimately determinative of the character of the relationship. I am not sure to what extent this analogy is legitimate. But at least it seems to have biblical warrant and also, somewhat to my surprise, possibly to say something about the doctrine of purgatory!

There is a third and final objection that I would like briefly to consider. When the eschatological fulfilment of man's participation in the eternal life of God is modelled in terms of a life 'after' death, at least some hope seems to be held out for those who, in their historical existence, know little or nothing of life, or freedom, or love; for the unloved child who dies of cancer; for the man or woman brutalized into egocentric despair by the relentless hostility of their surroundings; for those whose unloveliness seems due to the fact that they have never experienced a loving to which they could respond. On my account, what sort of hope could we hold out for people such as these?

As soon as one puts it like that, it seems to be the wrong question. Why should we be allowed the luxury of a vicarious hope? It is those without hope who need hope; those without love who need loving. There would be a kind of obscenity in diverting ourselves from the task of constructing the contexts in which such hope could be born by speculations which soothed *our* unease, but which achieved precisely nothing for those the squalor of whose suffering disturbed our tranquillity. That is the first point.

The second point is that attempts to articulate, to spell out, faith in resurrection must not be distorted into attempts to make sense of suffering and death. The gospel does not make sense of death, does not unravel the mystery of evil; it affirms that dying is the impenetrably dark face of coming alive. Once deprive Christian reflection on the mystery of man's participation in God's eternity of its dark centre in Gethsemane and Golgotha, and it is no longer in the light of Easter that we are seeing and speaking. If you 'leave Calvary behind', you move, not into paradise, but fairyland. Concerning the meaninglessness that is an irreducible component of all suffering, all inhumanity, all corruption, there is perhaps not much that we may legitimately *say*. But there is not a little that, in the Easter hope, we may discover the courage to *do*.

INDEX